MAO
ZEDONG

FREDERICK KING POOLE

MAO ZEDONG

15247

FRANKLIN WATTS
NEW YORK | LONDON | TORONTO | SYDNEY | 1982
AN IMPACT BIOGRAPHY

A GROLIER COMPANY

Photographs courtesy of:
Rene Burri © Magnum Photos, Inc. p. 14;
Culver Pictures: pp. 31, 47, 52;
United Press International Photo:
pp. 36, 67, 88, 93, 112

Library of Congress Cataloging in Publication Data

Poole, Frederick King.
Mao Zedong.

(An Impact biography)
Bibliography: p.
Includes index.
Summary: A biography of the man who transformed
China from a culture steeped in ancient traditions
into a revolutionary communist state.
1. Mao, Tse-tung, 1893-1976—Juvenile literature.
2. Heads of state—China—Biography—Juvenile literature.
[1. Mao, Tse-tung, 1893-1976.   2. Heads of state.
3. China—History—1949-1976]   I. Title.
DS778.M3P66 1982   951.05'092'4   [B] [92] 82-10905
ISBN 0-531-04481-5

CONTENTS

A NOTE ON CHINESE NAMES

Until recently the Chinese characters used to spell proper names were transliterated, or written, in our alphabet, according to a system known as "modified Wade-Giles." This system is still the most familiar to American readers, but since the mid-1970s, some writers in English have used a new system, called *pinyin*, which was adapted by the Chinese government.

In this book, all place names are given in Wade-Giles, following the style in most major newspapers, since the *pinyin* versions are unrecognizable. Also, following current newspaper practice, *pinyin* is used for names of people when it is close to Wade-Giles, as in Mao Zedong (*pinyin*) in place of Mao Tse-tung (Wade-Giles). However, Wade-Giles is used when the new version would be unrecognizable, as in the spelling for the name of Mao's last wife, Chiang Ching (Wade-Giles) instead of Jiang Quin (*pinyin*).

MAO ZEDONG

CHINA AT MAO'S BIRTH

1

The revolution that would be led by the tall, moonfaced man from the interior named Mao Zedong took place because by the time he came along the ways the Chinese had followed for thousands of years were not working. No one in the modern era had been able to solve the mounting problems of governing this nation that contained a fifth of the earth's population. China was the world's oldest continuing civilization, but its ancient form of government by scholars responsible to an emperor, who was said to have the "Mandate of Heaven," had become lax and corrupt. At the time of Mao's birth on December 26, 1893, bad administration of the country's resources had made starvation commonplace, and the nineteenth century had already seen armed insurrection.

Although larger by far than any other nation, China was being forced by smaller countries to bow before them. In 1894, less than a year after Mao was born, China suffered one of the most humiliating in a long series of blows to its prestige, authority, and self-esteem.

This particular setback came when the Japanese, long despised by the Chinese as mere imitators of their much older culture, attacked Korea. Korea was the last important Chinese dependency, meaning it was a country traditionally controlled by China, although not considered a part of the Chinese nation. Situated on a wide peninsula leading down from China's northeast coast, Korea has always been strategically important, but the Chinese military was so backward that it could not mount a serious defense. With superior arms, and modern military expertise, Japan easily made Korea its colony. And the next year Japan colonized Taiwan, the big island off China's southeast coast.

In the preceding years China's other dependencies had been falling fast. In 1860, in the far north, the Russians had taken Eastern Siberia. In 1862, in the south, the French had invaded Indochina (today's Vietnam, Kampuchea, and Laos), and were on their way to making it a French colony. Nearby Burma had fallen to the British in 1883. Thailand only managed to avoid colonization by playing off the French and the English, with China not a serious factor in its survival. Moreover, for centuries European powers had been entrenching themselves ever more deeply in other colonies all through the Far East—the British in India, for example, the Dutch in what is now Indonesia, and the Spanish (soon to be supplanted by the Americans) in the Philippines. By the end of the nineteenth century, however, the encroachment of the great powers on China itself had become even more alarming than the might of Western powers in other parts of Asia, and the loss of dependencies.

This encroachment had at first come as a surprise to the Chinese, who called their country the Middle Kingdom, meaning they considered it so important that it was the center of the world. They had expected all foreigners to recognize their superiority. China had been a major, and an unusually smoothly functioning, civilization since a thousand years before the Christian Era in the West. On the other hand, Europe, after the fall of the Roman Empire, was for centuries an area of backward, illiterate people, most of them living in tribal societies. All this time China continued to flourish, producing great philosophers and scientific thinkers, great poets, artists, and artisans. Its peasant farmers for the most part did not live very differently from their counterparts in the West. But its Imperial and educated classes lived a life full of refinement and splendor unknown to Europeans.

There was more than grandeur to the activities of China's leaders. China needed a sophisticated and smoothly functioning system of government because there was so much to govern. The country is vast, stretching some 2000 miles (3200 km) north to south and over 3000 miles (4800 km) east to west. Although active cities developed—as administration centers, markets, and ports—most Chinese lived on the land. Much of that land requires irrigation, meaning a need for cooperation and efficient administration to maintain the water systems. This is why, as the authority of the government broke down, food was so often in short supply, and parts of the country periodically suffered famine.

Although convinced of their superiority, the Chinese had not been unaware that there were other countries in the world. For hundreds of years there had been trade with Europe. But this was mainly because Europeans wanted fine Chinese products such as tea, spices, luxurious silk cloth and garments, and exquisite porcelain and lacquer ware. The Chinese found nothing they wanted in exchange from the Europeans except gold and silver. Europeans, like everyone else beyond China's borders, continued to be considered backward barbarians. The common Chinese word for a European or American was "foreign devil"—a term that lingers in some Chinese societies, as in the British colony in Hong Kong, to this day.

In the eighteenth and nineteenth centuries, when Europe and then America went through the Industrial Revolution, the West shot ahead of the East with new technology. Still, the Chinese remained uninterested in what was going on beyond their borders, and in anything alien to their ancient ways.

As early as 1742 an event occurred that heralded the new era China would be entering, and revealed the country's underlying weakness. A British sea captain, George Anson, sailed his ship up the Pearl River in southern China to Canton, which at the time was the greatest port in the East. Although he knew foreigners were not welcome at Chinese ports, he needed repairs and fresh supplies. The authorities in Canton refused assistance. But Anson, who only had one ship and 200 men, carried cannons and small arms such as had never before been seen in Canton. He announced he was prepared to destroy the city if help were not forthcoming. Immediately the authorities gave in and provided him with everything he had requested. The Chinese simply did not have the modern weapons needed to resist him.

THE OPIUM WARS

By Mao's time, such embarrassing encounters with the West were no longer isolated incidents, but rather comprised an overriding fact of life in a nation that was clearly losing the power to determine its own destiny. In 1839, British merchants, who had been looking for something to sell to the Chinese to balance their payments for Chinese goods, hit upon the powerful narcotic opium for which there was some demand in China. (Opium is better known today in the stronger form called heroin.) In their colony of India, the British planted vast tracts with poppy plants from which opium is made, but there was a major obstacle to using opium in the China trade. Because the Chinese wanted to avoid the problem of drug addiction, opium was illegal in China. But superior arms overcame the legalities of the matter. In a series of violent clashes, known to history as the Opium Wars, the Chinese were forced to allow the open purchase of the drug. More importantly, they were forced to make other commercial and even territorial concessions that encouraged trade with the Western powers.

With more and more opium available, drug addiction soon became a much greater problem throughout China than it ever had before, and to pay for the drug, China's treasury was being depleted. Increasingly more unwanted trade was forced on China. The trading countries were taking control of China's resources, and also exercising sovereignty over the parts of the cities where they operated.

Foreign trading colonies had been maintained for several centuries by the Portuguese in Macao, located at the mouth of the Pearl River, and on the big east coast island they called Formosa, now known as Taiwan. But their activities had been tightly controlled, and they had not been considered a threat to China's independence. Now, however, the British forced the Chinese to give them the island of Hong Kong and surrounding territory south of Canton, where they set up a full-scale colony. In all the major trading cities of the country, the British—followed by the French, the Germans, the Russians, and the Americans—seized sections in which the law of the foreign powers, not Chinese law, prevailed. These areas under foreign control became known as "concessions." Shanghai, which was to become China's largest city and most important port, was soon dominated by concessions.

THE DECLINE OF THE
IMPERIAL GOVERNMENT
Meanwhile, in the China into which Mao was born there were other factors causing further dissension and weakness. The Ching dynasty, the ruling faction or family that had controlled China since 1644, had never been popular. Its members, called Manchus, had originally lived in Manchuria, far to the northeast, beyond the 1500-mile (2400-km) Great Wall of China. Many Chinese had never fully accepted rule by the Manchus, and since the early days of the dynasty, illegal secret societies had worked to undermine the government. Sometimes these societies failed to draw a line between political action and outright banditry.

When the Manchus proved too weak to stop the foreign devils, the opposition grew bolder. Rule by law was breaking down. Bandits controlled large areas, and insurrections against the government became more common. Then, in the middle of the nineteenth century, there was a major revolt, known in history as the Taiping Rebellion. Taiping means "Great Peaceful Heavenly" indicating the religious overtones of the conflict. It was led by a Chinese Christian convert, Hung Hsiu-ch'uan, who claimed to see visions and said he was Christ's younger brother. Tens of millions of peasants joined the Taiping armies. They took over most of southern China, and their capital, at Nanking, became a rival to the Manchu's capital, Peking, in the north.

The West clearly did not want a strong China, not even under Christian leadership. When the government forces struck back against the rebels in 1864, they were helped not only by arms supplied by the West, but also by Western soldiers. They defeated the Taiping forces in one of the greatest mass slaughters the world has ever seen.

More and more Chinese became convinced that the West, which their ancestors had not taken seriously, was now invincible. And this belief threw the old Chinese ways into doubt. China had for millennia been governed according to a series of dicta laid down by the sage Confucius, who precisely defined relationships between men and women, family members, friends, masters and servants, and also between the governors and the governed. Since China no longer seemed able to ward off foreigners, more and more Chinese were asking whether the principles upon which the Chinese government and society were based were relevant to conditions in modern times. The Chinese had undergone a major loss of national self-confidence, and during Mao's youth it had become commonplace to look for new ways to meet the new challenges.

THE MAKING OF A REVOLU-TIONARY

2

Many of China's twentieth-century leaders came originally from the international coastal cities where they had become worldly through contact with foreigners in the concessions. But Mao Zedong was a man of south-central China, born 600 miles inland, which probably had something to do with his lack of interest in visiting foreign nations, and also his ability to win the loyalty of the Chinese peasant.

Indeed, there was much of the peasant in Mao. With a face that could somehow seem at the same time intense and placid, framed by tousled black hair parted in the middle, his appearance did not change greatly from adolescence to old age. He tended to grow fat when he was settled, but in his eighties his face was still almost unlined. He became unusually well-read for a man who was a successful politician and military commander, and he could match wits with the sharpest conversationalists. He was also capable of the rude, earthy remarks a shrewd peasant would make. He could stare down an opponent with a look of overwhelming intellectual superiority; he could also scratch himself in public like a crude farmer.

Although Mao's family were not rich, they were not exactly downtrodden either. Their house—now a national monument—was a sturdily built brick structure with several rooms. Unlike the majority of the Chinese, who lived close to the edge of hunger, even starvation, his father was a small landowner and merchant, prosperous enough to employ a few workers in his rice fields. The elder Mao was sufficiently well off to anticipate that his three sons and even his daughter, unlike most Chinese children of the time, might be able to better themselves through some advanced education.

The Mao family's farm was located in the village of Shaoshan Chung in the rice-growing northern part of Hunan Province. To the north of Shaoshan is the ancient provincial capital of Changsha, the administrative and market center for a large rural region. Farther north, snaking through the rice fields, is the great Yangtze River, which separates north and south China. To the south in Hunan are wild mountains, where bandits roamed in Mao's early years. Sometimes these bandits would, in the fashion of Robin Hood, give to the hungry poor some of what they stole from the rich landowners. Their exploits, reported in Shaoshan, captured the young Mao's imagination, as did the romantic adventure novels he read.

Chinese leaders tend not to lay out all the details of their personal lives in the manner of some leaders in the West, and for this reason, there are gaps in Mao's personal history. It is known, however, from his writings and his conversation that his father was a conservative man. He believed in traditional ways, and was particularly strict with Zedong, the eldest son. Very early the father and son began having verbal clashes, usually settled by Zedong's mother, who was a devout follower of the gentle philosophy-religion Buddhism.

The village school Mao attended was also old-fashioned. Nothing modern was in the curriculum. In the school Mao learned to read the old classical texts, and he complained later of becoming particularly bored with Confucius. He learned to write in the classical style. He was soon writing poetry in the old traditional way. He continued to write poems in the classical manner all his life, even much later when he vehemently condemned classical culture.

Because Hunan Province is a major thoroughfare between the north and the south, the simple village people of Shaoshan were not completely isolated from the major events of their time. Hunan had been a center of revolutionary activity during the Taiping period. There had also been many other upheavals in the region. As discontent with the current system rose, the tempo of conflict increased everywhere in China, and word of these far-flung events, too, got back to rural Hunan. At the turn of the century, in Mao's seventh year, the whole nation was shaken by the first concerted attempt to drive out all foreigners.

It was known as the Boxer Rebellion because its instigators, members of a secret society, practiced boxinglike calisthenic rituals, in the manner of the martial arts exercises called tai chi chuan, which they believed would magically protect them from bullets. With government encouragement, the Boxers lashed out at the West by attacking and killing Western missionaries and Chinese Christians in the countryside. In 1900 they were encircling Peking and appeared to be on the verge of conquering it.

The great powers quickly put together an international relief force 2100-men strong, which was dispatched to Peking to save foreign diplomats and merchants. The Chinese government ordered its own troops to help the Boxers by stopping the foreign force before it reached Peking; but the government troops, as had become the pattern when confronting Western forces, were swept aside with ease. The foreign soldiers took over Peking, and even entered the complex of palaces called the "Forbidden City," where China's rulers lived. There they looted with abandon. The West forced the Chinese to pay heavy reparations. The Americans later put their share into a scholarship fund for Chinese students.

In the next few years violence came closer to Mao's

home. First, during famine in Hunan, food was seized and riots over land ownership took place. The rioters were chased to the hills by government forces. And then in 1906 there was a large-scale secret society rebellion against the Manchus along Hunan's northern border. The rebels failed, and many were executed.

CONTACT WITH REVOLUTIONARIES

The year after this Hunan rebellion, when Mao was thirteen, he left the village school. For a time he worked in his father's fields by day and read everything he could get his hands on at night. For a time he lived away from the farm with a former law student and studied the classics with an old scholar who had come to stay in Shaoshan. He also worked as an apprentice to a rice merchant. But none of these activities satisfied Mao, and when he was fifteen he was ready for a larger world.

He had heard about a school in the nearby town of Hsiang Hsiang that had begun offering some modern subjects in addition to the classics. His father was against the move, but after Mao had shown his determination by borrowing money on his own, he was allowed to leave Shaoshan for the Tungshan Higher Primary School.

With three years of schooling lost, he was old for his class. At first, the other boys, many of them rich and garbed in fine scholars' gowns, made fun of this tall young man in rough peasant clothing. But Mao did well in his subjects and soon made friends with fellow students and teachers. They would talk together late into the night, and often the talk turned to the problems of China.

At the school everyone seemed fascinated with Japan, which had so quickly made the leap from an agricultural feudal backwater to the status of major world power, even winning a war against Russia. Many ambitious young Chinese, including one of the teachers at the academy, had gone to

In his teens, Mao (r.) was photographed
with his younger brother, Mao Zemin,
and his father and grandfather. The picture
captures the style and spirit of the China
Mao's revolution would overturn.

Japan to study. If that country could become so respected in the modern world, the teachers and students reasoned, so could the much larger, and potentially much richer, China.

The group at Tungshan was not calling for extreme changes in China, just for a better imperial government that would be more responsive to the demands of modern times. But these discussions about China's fate set Mao on the road to asking more questions and looking in other directions for answers. He was far from being a radical yet, but after two years at Tungshan he decided it was time to broaden his range.

He had heard about fine schools in Changsha, the provincial capital. It took no more than a day to get there from Shaoshan, but to Mao that trip must have seemed like an astounding adventure. So far he had never traveled more than a few miles from the farm where he was born, and he had never seen a real city.

Changsha had always supported an intense intellectual life. People there were far more in touch with the rest of China than people in the villages. At Changsha you could board trains to Canton in the south or Peking in the north, and steamers headed up to the Yangtze to connect with larger steamers following the route east to Shanghai. Because Changsha was so accessible to the great cities of China, it was inevitably becoming a center of revolutionary activity.

THE FIRST REVOLUTION
And so, in 1911, at the age of seventeen, Mao saw his first real city. He also read a newspaper for what was probably the first time. That newspaper happened to be the *People's Strength,* the organ of the Alliance Party, an illegal political party, that had grown up from a secret society headed by an American-educated medical doctor, Sun Yat-sen.

Mao had not had precise plans when he arrived in Changsha, but even if he had they would have been overridden by events. Sun, who despite his Western ways was first of all a Chinese nationalist, had already led a revolt against the government in Canton that had nearly been successful. He believed that change within the system was no longer possible, that China should not only get rid of the Manchus but get rid of all emperors; in order to progress, he said, China had to follow the Western model and become a republic.

In October of 1911, not long after Mao's arrival in Changsha, revolution broke out in many parts of China all at once. A few weeks after the revolt began, Mao joined the republican army. He served for only six months, and only as an orderly in a garrison, but it was a sign of his determination that he had enlisted not, like most men of his age with his education, as a member of a student militia but as a private in the regular army.

He did not stay in the army longer because most of China south of the Yangtze was soon in the hands of the republicans. In the north, however, Yuan Shihkai, the former commander of the emperor's forces, continued to hold sway. For a time it looked like stalemate, but in the summer of 1912, Sun and Yuan made a deal whereby Yuan would be named president of the new Republic of China in exchange for persuading the emperor to step down.

Meanwhile Mao, released from the army, had started to drift again. He studied law, then economics. He enrolled in a traditional school, but left the school to read Western philosophy and economics on his own at Changsha's recently opened public library. After a year he decided to take the stiff entrance examination for Changsha's rigorous teachers' training college, which prided itself on a curriculum that was both Western and Chinese.

He passed the exam, enrolled, and shortly emerged as a leader. Mao became secretary of the Students' Society. Although he showed no desire to go abroad himself, he was active in a group organized to send students to France and Germany to learn modern ways. He began writing articles for

Changsha newspapers about the need for social and economic change in China. And he was elected to command a students' army to defend their school when the city was threatened by competing warlords.

The warlords were generals who had abandoned the northern and southern armies and set themselves up as local leaders when the central authority of the Republic weakened and China became split again. The central government had broken down in 1915 when President Yuan almost succeeded in implementing a secret deal with the Japanese to make China subservient to Japan in exchange for Japanese support of a scheme he developed to revive the imperial system and name *himself* emperor. Garrisons throughout China revolted against Yuan, who died the following year, and the pattern for the next years was set. The warlords rose because with no effective central government for the entire country, there were vacuums to be filled.

China was very close to chaos by the time that Mao graduated from the college in 1918. But now, in touch with intellectual currents that were sweeping over the Middle Kingdom, he saw the years ahead not as hopeless, but as a time of exciting change. He wanted to be a part of the great events he was sure were coming.

Ordinarily a young graduate would have taken a job at this time, and Mao's father was furious when he heard his son had other plans. Mao was twenty-five years old, but so far he had never ventured outside Hunan Province. Now, he announced, he was going to place himself at what he thought would be the center of the action that would determine his nation's destiny. He would go to the capital, the traditional seat of the government for all of China: Peking.

BECOMING A COMMUNIST

It was now that Mao took the steps that would irrevocably link his future with that of all his countrymen. It was now that his thinking developed to the point where he believed only extreme change could save China. Such extreme change, he decided, could only be brought about through Communism. This political and economic philosophy, based on writings of the German Karl Marx, saw history in terms of the struggle of workers against capitalists. It was the philosophy of the revolutionaries who had recently taken control of the vast lands of the Russians. Communism meant the end of the power of the rich and privileged; it meant the communal ownership of all property. For China, it would mean an end both to the traditional ways of governing and to the recent experiments with Western-style republicanism and democratic thinking.

When he arrived in Peking, Mao secured a post as an assistant librarian at Peking University, the country's principal intellectual center. He stayed on the job only six months, but here he came in contact with the works of two influential men, Chen Duxiu, a literary scholar who had moved from Peking to Shanghai, and Li Dazhao, the university librarian. More than any others they were responsible for the formal founding, three years later, of the Chinese Communist Party (CCP).

It was also during Mao's first months in Peking that events were set in motion leading up to what was later to be considered a turning point—the day of massive student demonstrations, on May 4, 1919, that would be known as the May Fourth Incident.

What the students were protesting on this day was still another national humiliation. The Allied powers that had defeated Germany in World War I announced they would hand over German concessions in Shantung, a coastal province between Peking and Shanghai, to the Japanese, rather than give the concessions back to China. The May Fourth Movement came to describe what had happened to so many Chinese thinkers since the new republic had come asunder in 1915. It symbolized the rejection of liberal and moderate Western models of development in favor of the radical Marxist-Communist approach.

It also came to stand for the rise of a new generation that would be more aggressive than the old. The demonstrations were sparked by Chen Duxiu, but they were carried out by the young people. Two months later Mao wrote of his generation: "The world is ours, the nation is ours, society is ours. If we do not speak, who will speak? If we do not act, who will act?"

Mao was now a committed activist. For a time he returned to Changsha to help organize students, merchants, and workers to oppose the Japanese. Then he fled Hunan to escape the forces of a warlord governor who opposed the May Fourth Movement. Back in Peking in the winter of 1919–20, he immersed himself in Marxist literature that was being translated into Chinese. It was now that he made his commitment to Marxist Communism: "Once I had accepted it as the correct interpretation of history," he wrote later, "I did not afterward waver."

In the spring of 1920, after a change in government in Hunan, he returned to Changsha to become principal of a primary school. There in the autumn he put together a small local Communist organization. In the winter he began living with a serious young scholar, Yang Kaihui, a fellow revolutionary activist whom he later married and who bore him two sons. The next summer he went to Shanghai for a conference involving other local Communist groups—the meeting at which the CCP was founded.

Two years later the Communists joined in an alliance with Sun's new Nationalist Party in opposition to the much more conservative and militaristic government that was operating in Peking. Mao left his job in Changsha—the last job he would hold that was not strictly political—to devote himself to organizing again.

Now he began to see that there was more than one way to look at Communism. So far the CCP had been following the Russian lead, assuming its revolution, too, would be based upon urban workers—even though China had very little industry and consequently very few urban workers. Marx had shown contempt for peasants, yet peasants comprised 90 percent of China's population.

In the spring of 1925, while he was at home in Shaoshan for a rest, Mao saw peasants demonstrating in sympathy with rioters who had been shot by foreign police in faraway Shanghai. He became convinced the peasants could be as politically conscious as workers. Following the path that was being laid out by a few other CCP members, he turned his energies to organizing peasant associations.

So far the Communists had managed to work with the Nationalists under Sun Yat-sen. But 1925, the year Mao discovered the potential of the peasants, was also the year that Sun died. From now on the Nationalist Party was to be led by a stiff-backed military man, the former commandant of an important military academy, Chiang Kai-shek. And Chiang was soon to show how little sympathy he had for Communists.

RENEGADE

Later that year, still operating within the Nationalist-Communist alliance, Mao found himself in trouble with the Hunan authorities again. He moved to Canton, the Nationalists' base, and became editor of their newspaper, the *Political Weekly*. He also went to work as a teacher and administrator at the new Peasant Movement Training Institute, where peasants were given some education and taught methods of modern agriculture. Mao stayed with the institute until 1927, until after it had moved with the government up to Wuhan on the Yangtze. But at the end he was a renegade, and most of the young peasants he was training had joined him in opposition to the Nationalists.

It was Chiang who caused the breach in the alliance between the Nationalists and the CCP. In the spring of 1926, although he was getting help from the Soviet Union, he expelled most Communists from important posts. In the summer he launched his greatest undertaking to date, the Northern Expedition. The announced purpose was to sweep across China, do battle with the Peking forces and with the warlord armies, in order to unite China once again.

At the start, the Nationalist troops were well equipped and fired up with patriotism. They rapidly crushed the warlord armies in Hunan and the adjoining Kiangsi Province. Mao and others from the training institute followed behind them to organize the peasants, who were rising up, often savagely, against the old landowners. Part of Mao's mission was to help with the transfer of land from the owners to the peasants who worked it.

Trouble arose, however, because among the army officers were the most right-wing members of the Nationalist-Communist coalition. Many identified themselves with the landowners, and took the new activity among the peasants to be a blow to their own positions.

In March of 1927 Chiang's forces marched east to the great, foreign-dominated port city of Shanghai. Their job there was made easy by the workers who, organized by the Communists, in effect handed over Shanghai on a platter. Then a group of Chiang's officers met with a group of Shanghai's Chinese businessmen, and they were joined by representatives of the Western powers. The Westerners told the officers and businessmen that what they feared most was the destruction of business and property interests. They actually promised financial aid to Chiang if he would move against the Communists. A month later Chiang told his right-wing officers that they were free to attack.

During the next weeks something like 5000 Shanghai Communists were killed. A few prominent figures, including Chou En-lai, managed to get away, but the Communist Party in Shanghai had been decimated. And the slaughter did not stop there; Chiang gave his men the go-ahead to massacre

Communists in the countryside. The worst brutality took place in Mao's home province of Hunan where there was a governor who was intensely loyal to Chiang. Nobody knows how many people were killed in the province, but it was at least in the tens of thousands. Estimates were that of the 25,000 CCP members in Hunan, 15,000 lost their lives.

Looked at one way, it was a setback for the Communists, but from another perspective, Chiang had done what the Communists needed most to advance their cause. The peasants never forgot the horror perpetrated by the Nationalists. And many Nationalist officers, disgusted at what had taken place, deserted and went over to the Communist side. Among them were men who would become the top Communist generals, including Chu Teh and Lin Biao.

Mao himself had returned to Hunan just before Chiang unleashed his troops, and now, as one of the survivors, he was ready to fight the Nationalists for the first time. Four months after the massacre he led several hundred peasants into a craggy mountainous area in the southeastern part of the province. There, like the figures of the romantic novels he had read as a child, he became leader of an ever-increasing band of heroic outlaws.

THE YEARS
IN THE HILLS

3

For seven years after their break with the Nationalists the Communists were split into two different groups with different ideas on how the revolution should be waged.

One faction, based in Shanghai, still believed in a revolution on the Russian pattern that would start when the urban workers rose against their masters. This projected revolution was supposed to involve head-on clashes between the masses and the enemy's forces.

The other faction believed, with Mao, that the peasants were the key to the revolution. They advocated guerrilla warfare by an unusual regular army that would have the support of the people in the countryside. This army would confound the enemy by being able to blend into the countryside, moving among the peasants, in Mao's often repeated words, ''as fish in the sea.''

Officially the party leadership now supported the faction calling for a Russian-style urban revolution. The CCP's top governing body, its Politburo, remained underground in Shanghai, close to the urban workers and cut off from the rural people. Increasingly the party organization was dominated by men who had returned to China after studying in Russia. In Shanghai they tried without success to organize strikes, set up a program of sabotage, and encourage spontaneous worker uprisings.

From his base in the hills, Mao assumed, unofficially at first, the intellectual leadership of the rural side of the Communist movement. He also, despite his very slight formal military training, became the Communists' leading rural tactician. From high in the foggy mountains he announced his plan to turn the CCP temporarily into an army. This army would take in peasants, former Nationalist soldiers, even bandits who were ready to reform and follow his principles. The men, and a few women, would be trained to fight in hit-and-run attacks. At the same time, equal attention would be paid to their political training. It was a pattern that would be followed by the Chinese Communist military for many years.

Mao's departure from party doctrine inevitably brought him into conflict with the Shanghai Communists. Four months after reaching his mountain base he learned that the Politburo had stripped him of all party posts. For a time he tried to conform to the Shanghai version of how wars should be fought: he sent forces to confront warlord armies in pitched battles in southern Hunan. He was not only defeated, he temporarily lost control of his mountain base. Mao became more convinced than ever that he had been right in the first place.

In April of 1928 Chu Teh, one of the defectors from the Nationalists and an opponent of the Shanghai party leaders, arrived at Mao's base with his own forces. This brought the fledgling Red Army, as it called itself, to a strength of 10,000 men. Mao, the zealot, and Chu, who was much more relaxed and cheerful, would work well together in the years to come. They became so closely identified that later, when they began to control large parts of China, peasants when first hearing about them would speak of "Chu Mao" as a single, legendary man.

Mao and Chu worked out new orders for the army. The beating of men by officers was forbidden. Soldiers were not permitted to take anything from the people without paying for it. Any mistreatment of civilians was strictly forbidden and would be harshly punished. The army was forbidden to do all the things that were making the Nationalist and warlord troops so unpopular. The army was also to be the embodiment of Communist ideology. After each battle, a meeting would be held in which anyone could speak up, and there would be both criticism of others and self-criticism. Officers could be demoted if the men felt that they did not deserve their positions.

During the course of the year Mao continued to waver between following his own battle plans and those laid down by the leaders in Shanghai. Each time he sent his men out to fight pitched battles the results were disastrous. Again and again under fire he was being proved right about tactics.

There was still disagreement with his ideas. But late in 1928 the Sixth CCP Congress—meeting in Russia because no Chinese city was believed safe—elected him to the party's Central Committee, whose authority was just below that of the Politburo itself. It was at least tacit recognition that Mao was effective as a fighter.

THE KIANGSI BASE

Early in 1929, Mao decided to transfer his base east from the Hunan mountains to the green hills of Kiangsi Province, where the Nationalists and the warlords did not have so many troops. Also, the move put him out of reach of Hunan CCP officials, who kept nagging him to try conventional warfare.

It took weeks to make the move along icy ridges through the mountain passes. Half his soldiers carried spears because they did not have guns. Many died of starvation or exposure. Those who survived did so largely because, using Mao's favored guerrilla tactics, they overpowered Nationalist garrisons that lay along their route, capturing not only arms but food.

There were many reverses after they reached the new

Kiangsi base. Mao and Chu went through the experience again of following orders from above and attacking a city in force in the conventional manner. This time, the city was Nanchang, Kiangsi's capital. The Communists actually held Nanchang for a day, but were chased out when the predicted workers' uprising did not take place. They led a similar assault on Changsha, but this time Mao disobeyed orders and called off the attack when he saw success was out of reach.

It was during this time that two of the people who had been closest to Mao were captured by the Nationalists—his sister Mao Zejian in 1929, and his wife Kaihui in 1930. Both were promptly executed. But Mao did not slow down—either in his personal or revolutionary lives. Because he had been in the hills, he had not seen Kaihui for three years, and he was already living with a pretty young high-school girl, He Zizhen, another fervent party member, whom he now married.

Politically, if not militarily, Mao was doing well in his Kiangsi base. By late 1930 the Red Army controlled an area of 19,000 square miles containing three million people. Back in Shanghai there had been a shake-up in the CCP leadership, and Mao, who was somewhat more in favor with the new leaders, was placed on the Politburo. The leadership even decided to move out of Shanghai and use Mao's base to set up an opposition government for China. Mao's territory was becoming the center of all Communist activity; soon men styled as government ministers were arriving in Kiangsi.

At this time a group that had fallen out of favor in the party staged an anti-Communist rebellion inside the part of Kiangsi that Mao controlled. After several weeks of intense fighting he stamped out these new rebels, who had had aid from the Nationalists. Over the years he would say how important it was to convert enemies rather than eliminate them: "Cure the illness and save the patient" was one of his favorite phrases. In fact it was rare for him to pass a death sentence on a political opponent, but now he showed a ruthless side. He had hundreds, some say thousands, of the defeated rebels shot.

CHIANG'S "BANDIT-
EXTERMINATION" CAMPAIGNS

It was Chiang Kai-shek, rallying his armies as he never had before against the Communists in Kiangsi, who tested Mao's ability to survive. Although Chiang was still opposed by warlords and a warlordlike government in Peking, as well as the Communist guerrillas, he was suceeding in consolidating the power of the Nationalists. He established himself at the city of Nanking, midway between north and south China. To have his capital at Nanking was further proof of his legitimacy, he maintained, because through history Nanking at various times had served as an alternative to Peking as the imperial capital of all China. He was a long way from admitting that the Communist upstarts in the hills could be a real challenge to his regime.

Three times between the end of 1930 and the summer of 1931, Chiang sent massive troop contingents to encircle and wipe out Mao's forces in what he called, with a verbal sneer, "bandit-extermination" campaigns. First he sent 100,000 men against the Red Army, which now had 30,000 members. But using the hit-and-run techniques that had worked so well in recent years, the Red Army turned back all these attacks.

For a time Mao's star rose within the CCP. The part of Kiangsi his forces controlled was now called a soviet, which in CCP jargon meant an actual Communist state. There were other smaller soviets in existence in other parts of China. In the autumn of 1931 the largest conference the CCP had held opened in Kiangsi. Over 600 delegates came in groups from each of the soviets and elected Mao chairman of the new confederation called the Soviet Republic of China.

But as Kiangsi grew in importance as the seat of Communist power, Mao's star was going into eclipse. Later he wrote complaining that, "From 1931 until 1934 I had no voice at all at the center." By 1933, although he kept his title as chairman of all soviets, he had been removed from the top CCP policy-making bodies, the Politburo and the Central Committee. When Chiang launched his fourth extermination campaign the Red Army was led not by Mao but by the handsome and sophisticated future premier, Chou En-lai.

This fourth attack was somewhat halfhearted because Chiang was distracted by the Japanese, who had invaded Manchuria in the north. But by 1934, Chiang had signed a truce with the Japanese, leaving them in possession of Manchuria, and giving the Communists another point of contention with the Nationalists. Mao was already saying that all resources of Communists and Nationalists alike should be thrown against Japan, a course that would eventually give the Communists recognized moral superiority over the Nationalists in the eyes of most Chinese. But for now Chiang had made the extermination of the Communists, not the fight against Japan, his number one objective.

In the fifth campaign against the Communists, begun in the spring of 1934, Chiang had decided to take no chances. With the Japanese threat of only secondary concern, he was able to send 700,000 troops into Kiangsi, to take on a Red Army that by this time had greatly expanded. Aware that previous campaigns had not been properly planned, he turned to Nazi Germany for help and German officers were on the spot to advise him, both during the planning and during the fighting.

The Nationalists moved into Kiangsi slowly and carefully. After each advance they would stop, dig in, and build small forts. Soon the Communists were encircled by these forts, which were linked by rolls of barbed wire. Chiang was determined no Communists would get out alive. With the forts in place, shells from Chiang's heavy artillery weapons and bombs dropped by Nationalist aircraft were landing all over the Communists' territory. The Red Army had nothing with which to counter such firepower. By October only about 100,000 Red Army soldiers were left.

Their object now was escape. The bulk of the army was thrown against a point at the northeast of the Nationalist circle. After two weeks of desperate fighting, the Communists broke through. A few troops stayed back to harass the Nationalists, and most of the women and children from the base were also left behind. Nearly all of the soldiers who stayed back were killed, including Mao's own brother, Mao Zetan.

But the CCP's leaders were alive and on their way, some of them, including Mao, with their wives. The Red Army was making an exodus that would not only place Mao in the supreme power position within the CCP, but would mean the eventual doom of the Nationalists. This was the Long March, an event central to modern Chinese history.

MAO TAKES CHARGE

At the beginning of the Long March there was no clear destination. The Red Army moved to the northwest at first, heading in the direction of the eastern part of China's most populous province, Szechuan, a Nationalist stronghold. From the start there were constant skirmishes with Nationalist troops, but with Mao still outside the center of power, his tactics were not always followed. Red Army losses were heavy in the direct clashes with the Nationalists.

In November, the Red Army, motivated more by immediate survival than any set destination, was doubling back on itself, concentrating on keeping alive, with no fixed goal in mind. It moved south and then west through Kwangtung and Kiangsi provinces. In December the marchers again moved northwest, trekking through Kweichow Province as the sea-

*A rare photograph of Mao taken in the early 1930s,
probably before the Long March.*

sonal rains turned the roads to mud. Before the Long March began, the men had been fighting fiercely for five months, and then for two months they had been fighting while they marched. Now on a riverbank, the CCP leadership met to try to figure a way out for these hunted remnants of the Communist cause. Since it was Mao who, more than any other military tactician in any part of China, had been responsible for past successes, it was to him that the CCP now turned. He was, in effect, given command of the army.

On his advice, the marchers began to travel light. They had set out from Kiangsi trying to take everything with them, even printing presses. Now all machinery, everything except arms and food, was dumped at the wayside. Up to this point in the march the Red Army had been functioning rather like a conventional force. But quickly it was reorganized into small, unencumbered, fast-moving guerrilla units—the sort of forces that Mao knew were most effective. The Nationalists continued their attacks as the Red Army zigzagged through Kweichow. But Mao's forces, staying in small groups, staged guerrilla raids and kept Chiang's men off-balance. The Nationalists were unable to find the units that had been striking at them. The Communists had become fish in the friendly sea of the peasantry.

There were feats of heroism and also feats of cleverness. One night in December, Red Army men, using the element of surprise, stealthily climbed high cliffs overlooking a river. At the top they captured a Nationalist fort that had appeared impregnable. In the next month, carrying captured Nationalist banners, Red Army units appeared at the gates of Kweichow's provincial capital, Tsunyi. The Nationalist officials there, not realizing who these men really were, ordered the gates to be opened, and suddenly found their city in Communist hands.

By now the Red Army had come a thousand miles, and nearly a third of the marchers had already died—though most of the losses so far had come at the beginning when Mao's advice was being ignored. In any case, they were ready for a rest. While they rested, a crucial conference was called to decide upon the leadership of the CCP.

Mao was already the leader of the army; during this conference he became a great deal more. The old leaders, who in recent years had been pushing him further into the background, were stripped of their posts. And Mao was made chairman of the CCP—a position he held for the next forty-one years. It was by far the most important position in the party. As in other Communist countries, other men might at times have higher-sounding titles, such as president or premier, but the man who controls the party has the ultimate authority.

With his position consolidated, Mao continued to take a long view of history. He reaffirmed that the first most important job for any group that wanted to govern China was to defeat the Japanese, who were poised in Manchuria ready to conquer the nation. The goal of the marchers, Mao announced, would be Yenan in the rugged terrain of Shensi Province. Yenan was China's most backward area, located 2000 miles (3,219 km) to the north, well into the interior and just below the wild plains of Inner Mongolia. Here wild desert horsemen, descendants of the followers of Genghis Khan, still rode. Mao chose to go to Yenan because it would be a hard place for Nationalists bent on extermination to penetrate. It was also a place where the Communists might get control of lands the Japanese would have to cross if they were to realize their goal of spreading out from Manchuria across China.

ON TO YENAN
Under the leadership of the man who would come to be known as China's Great Helmsman, the Red Army split and marched back and forth across Kweichow, continuing to con-

found the Nationalists and inflicting heavy casualties on them. In March the Communists reached the border of eastern Szechuan, but Mao did not want to confront the troops Chiang had amassed in the region. Again he changed direction and turned south, heading for the town of Kweiyang, where Chiang had set up his own headquarters. The object was not a head-on attack but trickery. When Chiang got word the Communists were coming, he recalled troops from Yunnan Province to the southwest. Mao now led the marchers into Yunnan, which had become largely undefended. As the Nationalists were moving back into Yunnan in pursuit, Mao had turned north.

When the marchers reached the Yangtze, where Chiang had ordered all ferryboats destroyed, they searched and spotted one army ferry still afloat on the other side. Pretending once more to be Nationalists, they hailed the ferry, and once more got away with the ruse.

Now they pushed up through western Szechuan where Chiang, though he had some well-armed units in place, was not so strong. Ahead of the marchers, however, was another crossing at the Tatu River. To reach it they had to pass through territory controlled by hostile tribesmen, called the Lolo, who were so wild that no government forces had ever completely subdued them. To the Nationalists' astonishment, the Communists negotiated a peace and were actually led to the river by Lolo guides. The river crossing, however, was controlled by the Nationalists who had destroyed the planks of an eighteenth-century chain bridge across the Tatu.

The leader of the vanguard of the Communist marchers, Lin Biao, was one of the early Nationalist defectors. He worked out a plan with Mao and Chou En-lai to capture the crossing. Volunteers swung hand over hand across what remained of the old bridge. Many fell into the river, killed by fire from the machine guns of Nationalist soldiers at a guard-house on the other side. But some got close enough to lob grenades. In the course of a day, the volunteers had the crossing in their control.

From here on it was the terrain that was the main enemy, rather than the Nationalists. First, the marchers had to penetrate rugged mountain wilderness. When they came down from the mountains, in the far west of Szechuan, at the end of June, they met reinforcements, a band of Communists who had come from a soviet in Hupeh Province. But now the combined force had to spend weeks struggling through hundreds of miles of swampy grasslands. As they slogged along, members of a tribe called the Mantzu picked off stragglers with poison darts.

It was not until mid-August that the marchers had traversed the marshes and were re-forming. This time, however, the end was in sight. In September, advance scouts had reached the craggy terrain of Shensi Province. There were skirmishes with the Nationalist-controlled Muslim Cavalry from Inner Mongolia. But in October, after a final wild mountain battle with the Mongolians, the Communists were joined by horsemen from a soviet in Shensi. At last they were beyond Chiang's reach, for a time at least. The Long March had lasted one year and had covered 6000 miles (9600 km).

As the Communists settled in the town of Yenan in the Shensi Province, many, including Mao, set up simple quarters in hillside caves. When they counted up the survivors, no more than 20,000 of the 100,000 who had left Kiangsi a year ago had lived through the ordeal. The route of the Long March was lined with graves, dug as often for troops who had succumbed to fatigue, exposure, and starvation as for troops killed in combat. But for the Communists the important thing was that Chiang had lost his last good chance to wipe them out quickly. The Red Army and an alternative government for all of China were in place, with Mao at the helm of both.

Mao is shown here chatting with peasants in Yenan,
where his troops were based for over ten years
following the Long March and during the war with Japan.

GAINING RECOGNITION IN YENAN

For the first time in years, Mao, at the age of forty-three, was not on the run. As word about how Chiang had been outmaneuvered by the Communists spread through China, and as the legend of Mao's successes with Chu Teh took hold, Mao became a respectable statesman. No longer a man who could even remotely be identified with bandits, he grew more distant and formal, in the manner of a head of state. Foreign journalists, and then official representatives of the great powers, began journeying to Yenan to talk with him, sitting on the crude furniture of his cave dwelling. Many came away taking seriously his claim to the ultimate leadership role in China.

He began to lose the lean look he had had while organizing, while acting like a Robin Hood in the southern hills, and while on the march. He lived a simple life, if not a saintly one. The health of his wife, Zizhen, who had been badly wounded by shrapnel before the march began, declined, and she was sent to Russia for medical treatment. There she developed mental problems, and stayed on in an asylum. Mao divorced her—to the chagrin of some party officials, who said this was no way to treat a Long March heroine. He married another, even more zealous, Communist, a beautiful former actress from Shanghai named Chiang Ching.

The army regrouped and began to mushroom in size, taking in new recruits. They were joined by peasants from Shensi, where the Communists were redistributing land in an ever expanding area and also by more Nationalist soldiers, and previously unaffiliated patriots who had heard about Mao from afar.

The main opposition to the Communists was in the southern part of Shensi at the provincial capital Sian. The troops there were led by Chang Hsueh-liang, who was known as the "Young Marshal." Although his forces were officially allied to the Nationalists, most of Chang's men were unsympathetic to Chiang Kai-shek's cause. Many of them were from

Manchuria, where the Japanese had expropriated their lands. Both because they identified with the poor people who supported the Communists, and because Chiang did not seem to be making much of an effort to dislodge the Japanese, they tended to be more in sympathy with Mao than with the leader from Nanking. As things turned out, even the Young Marshal wound up on Mao's side.

Chagrined at how Mao's forces were flourishing, Chiang decided to make a personal visit to Sian in late 1936 to confer with his commander, Chang, and to rally the troops there. But he underestimated the feeling that was developing against him. In early December, the Young Marshal had Chiang kidnapped. Chang told the generalissimo, as he now styled himself, that he would be executed unless he called a halt to the civil war against the Communists and concentrated on fighting Japan.

During the weeks that followed, Mao showed great magnanimity. Despite what Chiang had done to his followers and even to his family, he knew that the generalissimo still enjoyed enormous prestige in much of China. Mao thought Chiang would be needed if the Japanese were to be stopped.

In an agreement worked out by Chou En-lai, who had emerged as the Communists' most effective diplomat, Chiang was released. The Communists even agreed to recognize him as the head of government for all of China, provided he kept his promise to stop fighting them and turn his forces against the Japanese. Under these terms, Chiang was allowed to return to Nanking, and the Red Army, on paper at least, became the Eighth Route Army, a force technically under Chiang's command.

THE TWO WARS AGAINST JAPAN
Six months after the kidnapping incident, Mao and Chou journeyed to a hill resort near Nanking to work out with Chiang the details of their projected war effort. It was at this very time

in the summer of 1937 that the Japanese struck. The Japanese were holding large-scale maneuvers in Hopei Province, where Peking is located, when suddenly the military practice turned into actual warfare. Quickly they captured not only Peking but all of Hopei, including the major port of Tientsin and the mountain pass at Nankou that had been protected for close to two thousand years by the Great Wall. With little opposition, they then moved southeast into Shantung Province, on into the central, fertile Yangtze River valley, and down into south China. They also pushed west into Shansi Province, and north into Inner Mongolia.

When they fought their way into Shensi, however, they were stymied by the Eighth Route Army, the Red Army. Mao let the Japanese advance without hitting them directly, but his men cut off their communications in the rear and annihilated isolated units. The Japanese were able to capture towns in Communist territory, but like Chiang and the Nationalists they could never move freely in the countryside.

Shortly after the Japanese embarked on this phase of their conquest, it became clear that the Nationalists and Communists, though officially united, were in what amounted to two separate wars. The Communists took the offensive. The Nationalists became almost passive.

The Japanese swarmed over Nationalist territory, moving a thousand miles up the Yangtze, capturing the major railroads of the north and the cities they served, as well as all of the coastal ports and much of the south. Chiang managed to hang on, although the Japanese announced confidently that they had defeated him. He retreated way back into the muggy remote reaches of Szechuan, where he set up his new wartime capital in the humid, fetid city of Chungking. There he waited, sure that China was too large for any nation to conquer completely. No plans for attack were made. His troops dug in for defense. He called for aid from the West, which never materialized in the amounts he had expected. He was ready to sit it out until somebody else brought down the Japanese.

And so the conduct of the war against Japan inside China fell to the Communists. The Red Army moved into an area comprising the great provinces of north China—Shensi, Hopei, Shansi, Shantung, and most of Honan. They took over a land area larger than that of Germany and France combined, and with a population of close to 100 million. Again, although the Japanese were able to hang onto enclaves in the towns, the territory as a whole was being governed from Yenan.

The Japanese, like Chiang before them, played into the Communists hands by behaving so brutally that they had no chance of winning the common people to their side. In July of 1941 they had tried the kind of encirclement campaign that Chiang had used in Kiangsi. They called their campaign the "Three Alls," meaning "burn all, loot all, kill all." The Communists escaped the circle, but much of north and central China became almost a wasteland, and the death toll was probably in the millions.

By now Chiang, still refusing to advance, had changed his mind about cooperation with the Communists. He ordered attacks on Communist units along the Yangtze, and proclaimed an economic boycott of the Communist area. But Mao had been leading a campaign to increase agricultural production, which, before the war was over, made his territory economically as well as politically independent.

In the last two years of the World War II the Western Allies tried to bring the two major Chinese factions together. To spur on the war effort, they renounced all the old treaties that had given them territorial and commercial concessions. But it was Mao's men who fought on, not the Nationalists. Even when his last surviving brother, Mao Zemin, was captured and killed under torture by the Nationalists, he concentrated on fighting the foreign invaders.

At the war's end, a million Red Army men were moving about Communist-controlled territory. And throughout all of China it was the Communists who were credited with opposing the Japanese, as well as with giving land to the peasants. The Nationalists were widely considered to have disgraced themselves by refusing to fight; moreover, they were identified by the peasants with their old oppressors.

Mao actually flew to Chungking in August of 1945, just after the Japanese surrender, in a futile effort to resolve his differences with Chiang. During the next year the Americans were sending emissaries to Yenan to talk to Mao, and to Nanking, where Chiang reestablished his government, hoping to bring the opposing factions of China together. But all the hopeful American mediators could accomplish was a truce that was frequently broken. With the Japanese out of China at last, both the Communists and the Nationalists were poised for the seemingly inevitable, and ultimate, clash.

THE TRIUMPH

4

Until almost the time that the final, full-scale civil war broke out, Mao had believed victory would come in a matter of decades rather than of years. First, he wrote, there would be a long period after the Japanese war in which the Communists would work with other factions, including the Nationalist army, landowners, and pro-Western industrialists. Only much later would the Communists actually rule China, he thought. But when the civil war came, it proved to be a rout for Generalissimo Chiang Kai-shek, a triumph for Mao's cause.

Ever since the Japanese surrendered, there had been clashes between Communist and Nationalist units, but it was Chiang who started the full-scale war. In July of 1946 he sent his armies into Manchuria, which—largely because the Japanese had recently developed it—had become the most heavily industrialized part of China, and hence a prime prize.

Fighting erupted all over China, and at the start Chiang looked powerful. The Nationalists held all of south China, the provinces in the far west, and much of the urban north. The Nationalist army outnumbered the Red Army—now called the People's Liberation Army (PLA)—three to one. It had five times the number of small arms possessed by the Communists. It also had the tanks, aircraft, and heavy artillery that the Communists lacked.

Often the fighting was intense, and the casualties were high. Some three million people would be killed before the war ended. Yet it lasted just over three years—a tiny period of time compared to the years the Communists had spent already as an independent armed force. It was also very little time when compared to the years of Japanese encroachment, or to the decades of postwar struggle within a coalition that Mao had anticipated.

There were turning points in the war that came with no fighting at all. The balance shifted as Nationalist officers and soldiers, frequently entire units, went over to the Communist side with their arms. The Communists did the bulk of their fighting with weapons that had been handed to them, abandoned or sold by soldiers discouraged with Chiang.

At the very start, most foreign observers had the impression the Nationalists were winning because they conducted visible mass movements of troops. But throughout the war Mao's guerrilla units, which were able to remain virtually invisible in the countryside, were running circles around the formal and cumbersome Nationalist units. The Nationalists would make what appeared to be spectacular advances. But the PLA would move in quickly and take the territory behind them.

Mao had no qualms about giving up territory of his own so long as what his men were doing contributed to the Nationalists' ultimate defeat. The important thing was to live to fight another day. Even when the Nationalists captured and temporarily held Yenan itself, he was not worried. "Empty cities don't matter," he said. "The aim is to destroy the enemy's army." And Yenan was "after all, only caves."

As the Nationalist soldiers became more demoralized, morale in the Communist units soared. Sometimes the troops would pause to celebrate with the friendly peasants. Often they would sing. One of the songs Mao—who always liked to hammer home lessons—taught them ran, "Keep men, lose land; land can be taken again. Keep land, lose men; land and men are both lost."

MOVING TO VICTORY

By the end of 1947 the PLA was on the offensive all over China. They were still fighting guerrilla actions, but they were becoming so successful that, for the first time, Mao saw an opportunity for the Communists to engage in conventional warfare effectively.

By the spring of 1948 he knew his forces to be so strong that he was throwing them against the Nationalists in full-scale battles. In a series of such decisive actions, he pushed the Nationalists completely out of Manchuria. Soon the pattern was being repeated all through the nation. The war was no longer being fought in Communist bases, but rather in Nationalist territory. By the autumn of 1948, the PLA, bolstered by Nationalist defectors, actually outnumbered the forces that remained under Chiang's command.

The PLA was ready to move on Peking. Communist units surrounded the half-million Nationalist troops in the Peking area. But, rather than stage a fight that would destroy the capital from which they expected a Communist government to rule, the PLA leaders bided their time. The forces they had encircled could do no further damage. They waited until near the end of the war, when Peking's commander, as they expected, surrendered without a fight.

With Peking encircled, the PLA was taking, one by one, all of the other principal cities of the north. Representatives on the scene from the Soviet Union urged caution, telling Mao that this was the moment to negotiate with Chiang. But Mao, confident now at the turn of events, was already sending troops across the Yangtze into south China.

In April of 1949 Chiang Kai-shek was forced to abandon his capital at Nanking, fleeing first to Canton. But by May the Communists had Shanghai and were closing in on Canton.

The leaders of the People's Liberation Army—
(l. to r.) Chou En-lai, Mao Zedong, and Chu Teh.

Five times during 1949 Chiang moved his capital, each time just a step ahead of the advancing PLA. Near the end of the year, he boarded a boat on the east coat that would take him to Formosa, the old Portuguese island colony which had been held by Japan and only recently returned to China.

Some two million refugees from the mainland moved to Formosa, today known as Taiwan. They included top Nationalist officials, members of the Nationalist armed forces, and many landlords and businessmen who feared the Communists. Savagely taking complete control of Taiwan from its inhabitants, Chiang proclaimed a new capital there, and for many years he claimed that those who now ruled Taiwan were the legitimate rulers of all China.

Even before Chiang's final retreat, Mao had quietly slipped into Peking and established himself in relatively simple quarters in one of the ornate palaces of the Forbidden City, the seat of emperors. On October 1, 1949, he stood on a platform—with Chu Teh, Chou En-lai, and other leaders and war heroes at his side—in the adjacent T'ien An Men Square. In a simple ceremony, watched by hundreds of thousands of victorious soldiers and Peking residents who had crowded into the great plaza, he proclaimed the start of the People's Republic of China.

MAO AND THE GREAT POWERS
In late 1949, when the Communists staged victory parades in China's cities, most of the weapons they put on display had been made in America. No armaments had come directly to them from America; these were captured weapons, and an indication of how important America's support had been to Chiang.

Mao could not understand how America could support Chiang even after he had been discredited in the eyes of his people. Mao had been hopeful that America would be friendly to the Communists once it was apparent that they had carried the brunt of the war against the common enemy, Japan, and were winning the allegiance of the Chinese people.

In the Far East any kind of negotiations, whether involving politics, government or personal affairs, are usually conducted with great courtesy and patience. Asians believe people lower themselves in the eyes of others by losing their temper, no matter what the reason. But in one of his last meetings with an American official before the civil war started, Mao could contain himself no longer.

"If you Americans, sated with bread and sleep, want to curse the people and back Chiang, that's your business," he blurted out. "Back him as long as you want. But remember one thing. China is *whose* China? It sure as hell is not Chiang Kai-shek's; it belongs to the Chinese people. The day is coming when you will not be able to prop him up any longer!"

Previously Mao had expected America would eventually support him. He had been so optimistic that at various times in Yenan he had tried to teach himself some English. But Mao had not taken into account what fear of Communism was doing in domestic American politics after World War II. As Russia conquered the Eastern European nations she was supposed to be liberating from Germany, Americans were becoming afraid of a powerful Communist bloc determined to take over the world. It did not matter that Mao had from the very beginning been at odds with the Russians. To most Americans, Communism was Communism—to be fought as well as feared.

At the same time, Chiang Kai-shek, and especially his U.S.-educated wife, had made many trips to America. They had solidified friendships with powerful American politicians, particularly right-wing Republicans, who were becoming more active in their support of the Nationalists. The fear of Communists had become so intense in postwar America that soon most of the American officials who reported that Mao, not Chiang, had the support of the Chinese people found themselves out of work.

From the end of the war against Japan until the defeat of the Nationalists, Chiang had received about three billion dollars in aid from America. Mao, who had received no foreign aid from any source and had fought with American weapons Nationalist soldiers had thrown down, was proud that he had been able to go it alone.

When the Chinese civil war was over, American statesmen bitterly accused each other of being responsible for "losing China." By this they meant losing China to Russia, to a Commiunist grouping that was thought in America to be monolithic.

In fact, though, Russia had been no great help to Mao. Although Moscow had expressed sympathy for the Chinese Communists, the Soviet Union continued to recognize Chiang's government as the one that represented the Chinese nation. When Chiang was forced to abandon Nanking, most foreign diplomats there knew the fighting would be over within a matter of months and most of them went home. Even the American ambassador departed. But the ambassador from Moscow had actually gone on Chiang's first move in retreat, accompanying his government to Canton.

And just as Russia counseled caution and negotiation at the very moment in the war when Mao knew victory was within his grasp, so had Russian advisers been at odds with Mao all through his days of organizing and fighting. From the first years of the CCP in Mao's youth, the Russians had never been happy with a revolution that did not follow their ideas of what a Marxist revolution should be. It was, to them, something like a religious heresy to base a Communist revolution on the peasant in the countryside rather than on the urban worker.

Still, once Mao was in Peking, Russia recognized his government as the true government of China, while the United States was taking the view that the real government of China was Chiang's on Taiwan. And America was able to use its influence both with its powerful allies and small countries to which it was supplying aid to keep up the myth that the Nationalists ruled China. America swung enough votes in the new United Nations to ensure that Nationalists from Taiwan officially represented Chiang in the organization, rather than Communists from Peking. Moreover, Chiang still had a powerful military force, armed by the Americans, training in Taiwan. His announced objective was to return to take the mainland by force.

Although Mao did not particularly like or trust the Russians, he felt that, if he was to remold Chinese society, he needed foreign friends to stand beside him. He felt he needed a strong ally to dissuade Chiang from trying a comeback. He also wanted economic aid from abroad to rebuild the industry and agriculture that had been destroyed during the Japanese and civil wars.

Late in 1949, in his mid-fifties, Mao finally went abroad for the first time. It was for an eight-week visit to the Soviet Union. He wrote later that he did not enjoy himself in Russia. Used to the refined cooking of China, he felt the meals in Russia were badly prepared. Furthermore, he felt now that he was the ruler of the world's largest country, the Russians should at least treat him as an equal, but he was often kept waiting by Soviet officials. He knew they looked upon him as a junior member of the Communist world. Nevertheless, he put aside his personal feelings. Before he returned home, Russia—which most Americans now considered their greatest enemy—had officially become Mao's staunchest ally. Mao and the Russians signed a thirty-year Treaty of Friendship, Alliance, and Mutual Assistance.

REFORM AND PROSPERITY

In the first years of Mao's leadership of China, at least through 1953, the changes he brought about were not nearly so radical as many outside observers had expected. At the beginning, the highest policy-making body in the country appeared to be an assembly called the Chinese People's Political Consultative Conference. There had been many groups in China besides the Communists who had not liked Chiang, and they were represented in this assembly. And in the first government, eleven of the twenty-four members who ranked as ministers were not members of the CCP. It was nothing like the Communist-Nationalist alliance that Mao had thought would have to precede the ultimate assumption of power by the Communists. But it was in many ways what Marxists call a united front government, rather than a purely Communist one.

Having taken care of foreign relations for the moment, Mao quickly set about the gargantuan tasks of reforming society and saving the people from poverty. Since nine out of ten Chinese, whose numbers were now approaching 600 million, were peasants, the greatest emphasis was placed on land reform.

The first step was to take land away from the big owners. It was the first time most Chinese peasants had ever had

*Chairman Mao Zedong celebrates
the first anniversary of the
establishment of the People's
Republic of China. At his side
is Liu Shaoqi, who later became
president of China and a leader of
the "pragmatists" who opposed Mao.*

such freedom to act against their oppressors, and for a time many ran wild in parts of the countryside.

Nobody knows how many Chinese were killed in these first months of the new regime, but it was believed to be in the hundreds of thousands. Most of the victims were probably landlords who had treated the peasants badly. Not all landlords were killed, however. Most were put on trial, made to confess their misdeeds, then forced to become farm workers. Yet, as is always the case in major, violent national upheavals, many people died for nonpolitical reasons. With so much killing going on anyway, it became a time to settle old personal feuds.

In the initial land reform program, landowners with medium-sized holdings were allowed, for the time being, to keep their land, but the estates of the biggest landowners were broken up. For the first time in their lives, most farmers now owned the land they worked. The government also put much effort into setting up efficient, centralized systems of food distribution. Until this time, as we have seen, mass starvation had been a part of Chinese life. Now the very threat of famine was virtually eliminated because food distribution was being planned on a national scale.

Liberating the poorest peasants from their overlords was a major break with tradition. Confucius had said servants should be faithful to their masters, as women should follow the lead of men. Right from the start of his government, Mao was nibbling away at the old Confucian principles that defined all relationships in China. He was taking the first steps in pushing people to transfer their first allegiance from family, friends, and masters to the Communist state.

In another dramatic series of moves, Mao also flew in the face of accepted Chinese practice by officially liberating women. One of the first acts of the government was to ban arranged marriages, long the fate of girls in the countryside. Chinese women were also, for the first time ever, given the right to own property. They were made equal to men under the law.

Just as Mao was transforming the countryside, so he was transforming the urban areas. Previously the major cities had been centers of trade where foreign interests held sway. With the exception of the people living in the heavily industrialized cities of Manchuria, urban dwellers had produced very little in return for the food they consumed, which was produced by the peasants. Now there was no foreign trade left, and Mao decreed that the cities, like the rural areas, must become productive. The new government promulgated measures to create new factories in every urban neighborhood in every city in the country.

In the cities there was no ancient social system comparable to the landowner-peasant system; therefore, there was no need to initiate social changes comparable to those taking place in the countryside. Many of the urban capitalists who remained instead of fleeing to Taiwan or Hong Kong now simply announced that they were Communists

For a time, many who stayed and swore allegiance to the new government were allowed to keep their factories. Others, who were considered the worst exploiters, were sent to work in the countryside along with the peasants, just as many of the surviving old landowners had been sent to the fields. It was part of a policy Mao called *hsai-fang*, which involved sending people to the countryside to learn from the peasants. The peasants in the new state were officially exalted above all other Chinese.

As the years unfolded, millions of city and town people went to live and work in the farming regions. Often they were sent as punishment, as in the cases of the rural and urban exploiters, and political figures who fell out of favor. But they also went as part of Mao's plan to keep the spirit of the revolution alive. Almost everyone—whether government official, factory manager, teacher, or student—who remained in good standing with the authorities was expected from time to time to go off and work in the fields, learning from the peasants.

Except for the formerly very rich landowners and industrialists, almost everyone seemed to benefit economically in the first years of Mao's rule. To the astonishment of many observers, who had predicted there would be chaos after Chiang fled, China began almost instantly to prosper.

It was not just that starvation was at last eliminated. Health services were inaugurated all over the country, with intensive training of paramedics, giving most people the first access they had ever had to medical professionals. Life expectancy suddenly became greater than in other Asian countries. And now almost everyone, child and adult alike, had access to schooling.

Industrial production, always pitifully weak under the Nationalists, was moving upward. Also, new bridges were being built across the great rivers. Railroads and other systems of transportation and communication were being rebuilt and expanded. It seemed to be the first time since Japan's rapid industrialization in the nineteenth century that a major Asian country was on the way to becoming an equal to the Western nations.

In the past, an emperor had been said to hold the Mandate of Heaven only so long as he governed well and gave his people a better life. Many Chinese, probably most Chinese, were coming to look upon Mao as a good emperor.

THE KOREAN WAR

After Mao took office, the last pockets of resistance to his new government were quickly eliminated. The big island called Hainan off the coast of Indochina was invaded and taken with few casualties. Tibet—which, like Manchuria, had not been a part of ancient China but had been part of the nation since the seventeenth century—was brought under the control of Peking. The British and Portuguese were allowed to keep the coastal enclave colonies of Macao and Hong Kong, because these trading colonies provided virtually the only source of foreign exchange funds China had. But, except for these two colonies and the island of Taiwan, the central government of China once again controlled all the territory it claimed.

Although Mao now wanted to put foreign affairs aside and concentrate on the country's economic progress, this plan proved to be impossible. In 1950, less than a year after the new Communist state was proclaimed, China was at war again. This war, fought on the Korean peninsula, would almost immediately influence the internal path the new China took.

China had no territorial claims on Korea. No one knows for certain if it was North Korea, which had been an independent Communist state since the Japanese surrender, or South Korea, a thoroughly capitalistic state, that set the war in motion through their threats against each other. It is generally agreed, however, that North Korea took the first overt military action. But whatever the reasons for the war, it was too close to home for comfort, Korea being an entry point to the industrialized Manchurian region.

When the fighting began and North Korean troops moved into the south at the end of June 1950, the United States hastily sent troops to help the South Koreans. At this time, the United States was able to gain the approval of the United Nations Security Council for a peace-keeping force to be sent to Korea. Because the Soviet Union was boycotting UN sessions at the time, the measure passed without the veto that might otherwise have been expected from the Soviets. To carry out the terms of the resolution, soldiers from many UN countries were sent to join U.S. troops under the command of the commander in chief of U.S. forces in the Far East, General of the Army Douglas MacArthur.

MacArthur successfully led his forces against the North Koreans, pushing them out of South Korea and capturing North Korean territory as far north as its 500-mile border with

Manchuria, along the Yalu and Tumen rivers. Although MacArthur was ordered to keep American troops well away from the Yalu, South Korean and other UN troops took up positions along the Chinese border.

From the Chinese point of view, the presence of these enemy forces, combined with the U.S. Navy's Seventh Fleet sailing in the Formosa Strait, was very threatening. Mao responded by sending a quarter of a million troops across the Yalu into North Korea. Forgetting for the moment about guerrilla tactics because the immediate threat of invasion seemed so great, he told his commanders to send the PLA into North Korea in waves. He knew he could not match the UN forces in modern, mechanized warfare, but, he said, China would overwhelm them with sheer numbers. The loss of life was immense. And again, as in past conflicts, the personal cost to Mao was high. Mao Anying a twenty-nine-year-old son born to him by his first wife, Kaihui, was among the casualties, killed when a command post inside North Korea was bombed. The Chinese army, however, succeeded in driving the UN forces out of North Korea and capturing the South Korean capital of Seoul in January 1951.

At this time, General MacArthur believed that the only way to win the war was to attack the Chinese base across the Yalu. He had considerable support for this plan, which involved using Chiang Kai-shek's Nationalist Chinese army in an attempt to cripple China's military power. MacArthur and his supporters believed this move would help contain the spread of Communism in the Far East. But the U.S. government was determined not to get into a full-scale war with China. President Harry S. Truman rejected MacArthur's plan, and when the general continued to press his views, he was relieved of his command. Chiang was kept away from Korea, and the PLA fought the Americans and their allies to a standstill. The war ended in lengthy negotiations that placed the North and South Koreans back where they had started before the war began.

Mao's prestige was increased immeasurably by his action in the Korean conflict. He had taken on the most powerful country in the world, fought it to the point where it did not want to fight further, and emerged with no loss of territory. Never again, the world was told, would China bow to a foreign power. More and more nations, including important non-Communist European nations, were now officially recognizing the regime in Peking. And more and more people throughout the world—particularly in poor, undeveloped countries that were gaining independence from the colonial powers—were looking to the Chinese for leadership.

Usually when a country goes to war against a foreign power one early result is a curtailment of liberties at home, and China during and after the Korean War was no exception. Intellectuals who discussed ideas that wavered from the thoughts contained in Mao's writings were condemned at mass meetings, and sometimes forced, in the most humiliating way, to confess their errors publicly. This was in keeping with Mao's stated policy of curing the illness but saving the patient. Many of these intellectuals found themselves bending over rice plants. The patient, however, was not always saved. Others whom Mao suspected of being in opposition were killed in harsh crackdowns in the cities.

Freedom as it is known in the West was not a priority on the Communist agenda. The prime goals were to eliminate hunger, then build up the nation, and at the same time reform and change the very nature of the society. In the days of the emperors, and in the time of Chiang and the warlords, no tradition for free speech had ever developed.

Yet just before the Korean War the people had begun to enjoy more freedom of expression than they had previously known. The war showed how shaky were the foundations for such liberty.

Mao was tightening his grip on the country. Although he believed in civilian rule, he had by now given considerable political power to the PLA; many soldiers held civil administrative positions. Although he had started out permitting regional administrations to exercise a great deal of authority, he was now transferring power from the provinces back to Peking, in order to maintain his own control of the country.

Like many an emperor in ancient days, he began to worry that he was getting out of touch with what was happening in his domain. To stay in touch, he frequently appeared in public and took part in give-and-take with people attending mass meetings. But still he feared isolation. At one mass meeting in the middle of 1953 he complained that, "Practically nothing comes to my ear in Peking." Like the emperors before him, he began sending out spies. Members of a special unit that had developed from his personal bodyguard were sent to the villages to find out what people were thinking and report back to him.

If he was starting to act a little like an emperor, it was because he was determined to do everything in his power, at whatever the cost, to maintain control of China and of his revolution.

In revolutionary Communist Russia there had been three key figures: Marx, the man who supplied the theory; V. I. Lenin, the man who led the revolution that brought the Communists to power and presided over the new state in its first years; and Joseph Stalin, who ruled for decades with a firm, often brutal, hand.

By working out his own theory of Communism based on the peasantry, helped by members of a regular army that melded in with the people, Mao had been his revolution's chief theorist. In effect, he was the Marx of China. By leading the revolution, he had also become China's Lenin. And now, using his own theories of constant struggle—in effect constant revolution—that he had been working out, he would rule, often harshly, for decades. His regime may not have been as brutal as the Soviets', but, in addition to being China's Marx and Lenin, Mao was becoming something like China's Stalin too.

THE STRUGGLE RESUMED

5

Visitors to China in the mid-1950s saw a country that, while obviously not rich yet, was adequately fed and apparently content. The People's Republic was tackling its problems. Food production was increasing; industrial capacity, though still no match for that of Japan and the Western powers, was expanding; transportation and communications facilities were being extended and improved. The great majority of the people enjoyed a better life than they had ever known.

China seemed both peaceful and conciliatory. And this was also the tone being set in its foreign affairs as conducted by Chou En-lai. Chou was one of the key negotiators at the 1954 Geneva Convention that ended the French war in Indochina. And he was the star of the historic first conference of nonaligned nations, held in 1955 in the gentle hills of Indonesia's Bandung.

China was encouraging revolutionaries in many of the underdeveloped, nonaligned countries, the so-called Third World nations. But although Peking occasionally sent financial support, most of the support was moral, no more than words of encouragement and brotherhood. After Korea, China never intervened with troops in any other country's affairs.

And yet China was not so serene as it appeared at first glance. There was bitterness left over from the crackdowns on dissidents that had taken place during the Korean War.

And people who did not believe in Mao's version of Communism now found they did not have a role to play in what modern China was becoming. In September of 1954, Mao announced tersely that there would be no more participation in government by non-Communists. "The force at the core leading our cause is the Chinese Communist Party," he said. By now all ministers who were not CCP members had been replaced.

Although he served as president of the People's Republic as well as chairman of the CCP, Mao still took time off to retreat to the countryside from time to time to think and to write. He did not believe that the end of the civil war was the same thing as attaining all his revolutionary goals. Increasingly it became clear in his writing that to him Communism meant constant struggle—in effect, that there was no end to the revolution. There would be periods when, as at this time, all seemed placid on the surface of China. But these periods were deceptive.

Mao feared complacency would undermine the goals of his revolution. From now until his death the country would go through struggles and upheavals that he himself set in motion. The need for what Mao considered correct thinking would take precedence over the need for material progress.

THE HUNDRED FLOWERS
CAMPAIGN

Mao was so confident in his ideas that for a time he seemed to believe that if he allowed freedom of expression all Chinese thinkers would come to share his views. If the people, particularly the intellectuals whom he often distrusted, were allowed to debate ideas openly, he thought, they would support those ideas that contributed to the revolutionary goals he had decided upon. Thus in 1956 he made one of his famous statements: "Let a hundred flowers bloom." And he added, "Let a hundred schools contend." What he meant, he explained, was that if ideas were to bloom like flowers, they must be given the proper climate. The proper climate, he said, was one of free debate. He was confident that only ideas within the framework of his own thought would survive open discussion. He was so confident that he decreed that just about anything could be printed in China—even transcripts of broadcasts put out by the Voice of America, even speeches made by Chiang Kai-shek.

But before very long Mao was complaining that the intellectuals had let him down. Far more dissent came into the open than he had expected. For example, students in Hunan held demonstrations carrying placards that said, WELCOME TO THE NATIONALISTS! and WELCOME TO CHIANG KAI-SHEK! And many intellectuals began questioning the very foundations of Mao's system of government. One wrote, "China belongs to 600 million people. It does not belong to the Party alone."

In addition to what, to Mao, was surprising criticism from intellectuals who had been given a chance to speak, there was new opposition developing among the CCP figures whom the intellectuals opposed. Important CCP leaders thought Mao had become too lenient—or possibly that he had, deviously, launched the Hundred Flowers campaign simply to catch them off guard. Liu Shaoqi—who would soon be president of China and would eventually oppose Mao openly—was one of the critics within the CCP. He let it be known that he felt the opening to free speech was dangerous; it could, Liu said, seriously undermine the CCP's authority.

Shortly after Mao made his Hundred Flowers statement, the CCP held its first congress since 1945. In 1945, Liu had delivered a report in which he mentioned Mao's name 105 times, and the constitution adopted in 1945 stated that the CCP would be "guided by the Thought of Mao Zedong." That phrase was stricken from the constitution adopted by the 1956 congress, and in 1956 Mao's name was mentioned by Liu only four times, an indication that Mao's prestige was at a low point.

Whatever was really behind the Hundred Flowers campaign, Mao had changed his mind by early 1957. He made a speech in which he distinguished between the kinds of differences in thought—he called them "contradictions"—that could be freely discussed and those for which discussion was forbidden. "Nonantagonistic contradictions" could be debated, he said. An example was the conflict, or "contradiction," in what it was felt a soldier should do. It was in the interest of the individual to live, but in the interest of the state to place a soldier in a position in which his death was likely. On such subjects there was room for debate and compromise. However, there were "antagonistic contradictions" that were beyond the realm of legitimate discussion, he said. An example was the conflicting interests of capitalists, who believed in private ownership, and Communists, who maintained communal ownership was best for the people.

Mao seemed to be splitting hairs now when he described what could be spoken freely and what could not. It became clear that he really had little use for free speech. Professors and students who had spoken up after his Hundred Flowers announcement were now silenced, and sent off to work side by side with the peasants. Still, any opening at all to free speech in a society without a tradition for free expression was daring. And so China was profoundly shaken by the Hundred Flowers campaign.

If one trait characterized Mao in the last two decades of his life and rule, it was his daring; China would be shaken many times more while he lived. In the name of revolutionary struggle, he was continually taking his countrymen, and the world, by surprise with his fast zigzags in policy.

THE RIFT WITH THE SOVIETS
One of the conflicts coming to a head was in the area of foreign policy. During the 1950s Mao was rethinking what should be the role of the Soviet Union in Chinese affairs.

From the first days of the CCP, Mao had been at odds

with the Soviets on a whole range of policy matters because of the new, peculiarly Chinese, theories of Marxist revolution he developed. He had also turned against the Soviets because, while encouraging the CCP with words, they had in practice given a great deal of support to Chiang. Later, during the Korean War, the Soviet Union had been content to let the Chinese do all the fighting in support of the Soviets' Communist allies in North Korea. It is true that the Soviets supplied guns and ammunition, but they did the supplying as armaments merchants. The Chinese eventually paid for the Soviet war matériel they used in Korea.

Now, in 1956, at the very time Mao was launching his Hundred Flowers campaign, the Soviet Union's earthy and outspoken premier, Nikita Khrushchev, began making new policy statements that were profoundly disturbing to Mao. Khrushchev denounced the harsh policies of the USSR's long-time leader, Stalin, who had died three years earlier. He particularly criticized Stalin for running the country as a one-man show, for letting what he called a "cult of personality" grow up around himself. Previously the official Soviet line had been that Stalin was virtually infallible. Now Khrushchev was saying just the opposite. Millions of people had died because of Stalin; and because of his policy of spending so much on arms, the Russian standard of living was poor.

Mao had often been out of sympathy with Stalin; and he had never been so brutal as Stalin, whose policies had led to the deaths, in peacetime, of millions of Russians. Yet Stalin's personality cult was a particularly touchy subject with Mao. Mao would often denounce what the Chinese called the "rare genius" theory of history, the theory that one man, as in the case of Mao himself, could be indispensable to a nation. But a cult of personality had most definitely grown up around Mao, and this attack on Stalin now sounded to Mao like an attack on himself.

Even worse from Mao's standpoint was Khrushchev's announcement of a new policy of "peaceful coexistence"

The warm welcome Mao received from
Soviet Premier Nikita Khrushchev on his trip
to Moscow in 1957 hid the widening disagreement
between the two Communist leaders.

with America. Khrushchev was aware that Russia could not become a thoroughly developed nation if it spent most of its money on arms, but to Mao this amounted to betrayal. Khrushchev's number one priority was friendship with the very people who had killed Chinese in Korea and were still supporting his archrival, Chiang Kai-shek. It seemed to Mao that Khrushchev, with his new friends in the West, was now more than ever determined to treat China as an inferior power.

In 1957, Mao made his second, and final, trip abroad to attend an international Communist conference in Moscow. There he made it clear that the Chinese were taking a different course than the Soviets. "The East wind prevails over the West wind," he proclaimed. He meant that eventually Communism was going to overcome Western imperialism in the world's developing nations, an idea that flew in the face of the new Soviet policy of cooperation with the West. His statement was also taken to mean that Communism from the Far East, meaning China, was the kind that would prevail—not Soviet-style Communism.

Mao began actively advocating that wars be fought in the Third World against those who supported Western interests. He still did not plan to send troops to fight these wars, and usually China did not even give financial aid. But with the largest nation in the world favoring limited wars, there were likely to be more of them. The Soviets feared that small wars such as these could lead to the major nuclear war they were so anxious to avoid, and this belief put them still more at odds with Mao. They were hardly reassured when Mao announced that he did not consider nuclear bombs such potent weapons. If they were dropped on China, he said, half the people would survive and the struggle against the imperialists would be carried on.

For a time, Mao was actually able to get Khrushchev to backtrack somewhat from his gestures of friendship to the West. However, Mao felt that China was becoming increasingly isolated from the rest of the Communist world. It was becoming clear that, by not following the lead of the Soviet Union, Mao placed China's interest ahead of what Moscow considered the interest of Communism worldwide. He was showing himself to be more a Chinese nationalist than an international Communist.

In addition to his ideological differences with Moscow, Mao was also becoming increasingly unhappy with the political results of his alliance with the Soviets. Russia had been niggardly in its foreign aid. There were, it was true, over 10,000 Russian technicians helping with China's development programs, such as water control projects and new bridges; but the aid Russia gave China was only a fraction of what America, and even European countries, were giving to many small Third World nations.

In late 1959, when Khrushchev was in Peking to confer with Mao, the rift came into the open. The occasion should have been a happy one, for all China was celebrating the tenth anniversary of the People's Republic. Later, however, Khrushchev told of "a chill that I could sense as soon as I arrived." Mao's wife, Chiang Ching, was to describe the Soviet leader's visit as "tedious and painful." In the course of their talks, Khrushchev infuriated Mao by speaking of the Soviet Union and the United States as two nations that had a special mission to maintain world peace. Khrushchev brought up an old request to set up radio facilities in China for the use of the Russian fleet in the Pacific. "For the last time *no*," said Mao, adding, "I don't want to hear anything more about it."

In the months that followed, they kept jabbing away at each other. At one point Khrushchev said the Soviets had only wanted to help but had been insulted by drunken Chinese. Mao complained that Russians who had come to China to help the Chinese always kept secret the most important information and development plans that China needed. Suddenly, in the middle of 1960, Russia recalled all of the Soviet technicians who had been working in China.

For a time the Russians and Chinese kept up talk of their

alliance even as they continued to hurl barbs at each other. But by late 1962, Mao was denouncing the Soviets as "revisionists," meaning they had deviated from the true Communist ideals. The word "revisionist" was always his ultimate insult and condemnation of people whom he felt had betrayed the Communist cause.

Henceforth there would be no cooperation between the Communist parties of the two countries. To add insult, Mao began sending aid to the tiny Eastern European nation of Albania, which had defied Russia by saying the Chinese were the true Communists. America was still considered an enemy, but in the future Mao would repeat over and over that the Communist Russians were even worse than the capitalist Americans.

THE GREAT LEAP FORWARD
While relations with Moscow were growing worse, Mao had embarked on yet another of his daring turnings at home. Partly to show the Russians he did not need them, and partly to stir his countrymen from the complacency he always feared would subvert the Chinese revolution, he announced in early 1958 what he called the "Great Leap Forward."

The Great Leap Forward was intended to be a crash program that, virtually overnight, without foreign aid but by the will of the Chinese people, would make China the equal of the industrialized powers. It was an anti-intellectual program in that Mao said the old intelligentsia, and the trained bureaucrats who implemented government programs, were no longer needed. A new intelligentsia, he said, would somehow emerge from the masses in the new rush to development.

The Hundred Flowers campaign had apparently been intended more as a way of stirring up the people than a real opening to free speech. Many suspected the Great Leap also had upheaval, at least as much as its stated goals, as its true objective.

There was something more like religious fervor than practical development behind Mao's concept of the Great Leap. Each time China was set on a new course, wall posters containing slogans would suddenly appear throughout the nation. Among slogans that came with the Great Leap were: "The achievements of a single night surpass those of several millennia"; "We shall create a new heaven and earth for man"; and "We shall teach the sun and moon to change places."

In the summer, another CCP congress was held. Unlike the congress two years earlier, when Mao had stayed in the background, he now dominated the proceedings. "When we look at the stars from the earth, they are in heaven," he told the delegates. "But if there are people in the stars, when they look at us wouldn't they think that we are in heaven? Therefore I say that we live in heaven as well as on earth."

In his writings at this time, as well as in speeches to the congress delegates and in speeches delivered before mass meetings, Mao made clear the principles that motivated him. Constant change was always needed, he said, because change was a fact of life. Trying to achieve balance was a waste of time because imbalance was a natural state. To be creative, you had to throw everything off-balance. If the system seemed to be functioning smoothly, it was probably a sign of a lack of creativity.

To mandate change from above was never enough, he said; harking back to traditional Chinese philosophy, he underlined the importance of sincerity. No change could come unless the people were stirred up, unless they were made to want change sincerely.

Furthermore, in Mao's view, the inevitable struggles that would come when the people were stirred up would result in a kind of purification. The men and women of China would be made better by struggle.

Again and again he emphasized that such purification,

such improvement, would never come from what trained experts did at the top. It was the masses, the fervent amateurs, not the professional planners, who should, and would, lead the way. It was, thus, that new leaders would emerge from zealous struggles to create the new army of intellectuals that he expected.

He was making wildly optimistic predictions about the practical results of the Great Leap. In heavy industry China continued to lag way behind the world's industrialized nations; but now Mao, in the most publicized part of the Great Leap, announced that China's steel output would rise eight times in the next fifteen years. China would be producing more steel than Great Britain, he said, and Chinese-made cars would by then have replaced the man- and animal-powered vehicles that still dominated Chinese roads and streets.

To the astonishment of China's government planners, Mao said China would become a major steel producer not by building great blast furnaces but by erecting very small, homemade blast furnaces in every backyard. People of all ages were told they should collect scrap metal for home smelting. Soon in many parts of China, there were chains of home-built furnaces, stretching hundreds of miles. It was not steel that these jerry-built plants turned out, however, but much less refined forms of pig iron, which is of little use in modern manufacturing. And in any case the production was only a fraction of what Mao predicted.

The same pattern held true in all areas in which the Great Leap was supposed to send production soaring. At first it was claimed that by the end of 1958 production of food grain—rice and wheat—had reached 375 tons (337.5 m t), up 102 percent over the previous year's production, and cotton had reached 3.35 million tons (3 million m t), a 104 percent rise. On this basis, goals of 525 tons (472.5 m t) of food grain, and 5 million tons (4.5 million m t) of cotton were set for 1959. But in 1959, Chou En-lai made a report in which he admitted the figures had been wrong. Actually, Chou said, only 250 tons (225 m t) of food grain and 2.1 million tons (1.9 million m t) of cotton had been produced in 1958. And he said the results had also been much lower than originally announced in such areas as coal mining, construction of water control projects, energy production, and production of fertilizer.

The people had responded with what appeared to foreign observers as genuine enthusiasm as they plunged into Great Leap undertakings. But enthusiastic amateurs proved to be no substitute for skilled planners. For example, people all over the country had thrown themselves into a massive effort, ordered by Mao, to eradicate pests—in particular rats, flies, mosquitoes, and also the sparrows that ate seeds. But sparrows also eat insects, and the immediate result of the attack on sparrows was destruction of crops by insects.

There was no famine of the kind known in the old China, but in 1959 there were more people in China going to bed hungry at night than there had been since the war years. It was clear that Mao's characteristically bold Great Leap Forward had ended in failure. It was also true that he had succeeded again in putting the whole country off-balance.

THE COMMUNE SYSTEM
The medium-sized private farms that had remained after the initial assault on the big landowners had gradually been eradicated. And so, for all practical purposes, had the small farms that had been carved out of the great holdings that had been disbanded. By the late 1950s most farmers had become members of cooperatives. This meant that, rather than working individual holdings, the residents of entire villages were working the surrounding fields together. Now, along with the Great Leap, Mao pushed communal farming a crucial step further. From now on the people would live on what are known as communes.

By now some communes had already started up in certain parts of the country, and won Mao's approval. The idea behind a commune was to combine at least three, sometimes more, cooperatives. The system would mobilize all the people over a large area, supposedly putting them to work where they would be most effective, which could mean working and living far from their homes. In 1958, Mao ordered that everybody in the countryside join a commune. Soon there were some 500 milion people on some 24,000 communes. Many communes held about 5000 or 6000 people, many were as large as 30,000 or 40,000, and some had populations in the hundreds of thousands.

The changes expected of the Chinese peasant in the commune system were extreme. The theory was that the people should not only work together, but also participate completely in a communal way of life. The role of the family would become less important. The children were to be raised primarily in schools. The workers were to live in sexually segregated dormitories. They would eat in mess halls. They would give up their homes and all other forms of private property. Obviously China's traditionally closely knit family units were not meant to survive these changes.

Some of the announced changes were hastily put into effect. Already men and women were dressing in asexual workers' garments, almost always a dull shade of blue. It was the regimentation expected of commune life, along with the appearance of the farm workers, that caused a number of foreign journalists to coin a new analogy: China, they said, had become a nation of blue ants.

The commune system, however, was never taken so far as Mao's statements indicated it had been. If everyone had gone to live in dormitories, it would have meant tearing down all the individual houses in villages all over China. But visitors noted that China was still a nation of villages. Most people, in fact, continued to own the homes they lived in. The houses might be old and cramped. It was common for some family members to sleep on the cookstove at night because there were not enough beds to go around. But these homes were invariably neat and clean inside, and freshly whitewashed outside. The people living in them were hardly blue ants, loyal only to the state. They were living, still, in families. On some communes, however, dormitories actually were built, and on most there were communal mess halls. There was, however, much grumbling about these alien living facilities.

Eventually the emphasis would be not on the commune as a whole but on small units, called production brigades, which usually had no more than a thousand members. And in time the emphasis would be switched to even smaller units, known as production teams, containing about 150 or 200 members. Later, on, when it became possible to raise more questions in public, it became clear that the communes were simply too large, that farming was much more productive when the emphasis was on smaller units, and also when peasants were allowed to grow some produce in private plots that they tended outside the hours of their communal workdays.

There were other problems, as well, which caused increasing opposition to Mao's policy. In pushing the commune system, Mao was actually giving more power to the professional planners against whom he so often railed. They were allowed to direct the nation's agricultural effort on the basis of theory, rather than on the practical experience of the peasants. Advice from veteran farmers who knew local conditions was often ignored in the late 1950s. In addition, much of a farmer's workday was wasted by the necessity of traveling great distances in trucks or buses to work unfamiliar fields. Young party officials who came to the farms from Peking often gave bad instructions, such as insisting on deep plowing in places where the soil was suited only to shallow plowing. Often when such mistakes were made, there was no one around to give good advice, since the farmers on the scene came from so far away that they knew no more about local conditions than did the young officials who had come from the capital.

During 1959, Mao was already backing away from his hard orders about communal living. He was allowing the unpopular mess halls, and the few scattered dormitories, to be closed down. People were being sent back to the fields they knew that were close to their homes.

MAO IN RETREAT
At no time did Mao relinquish the chairmanship of the CCP, the structural source of his power. And he never fully removed himself from the center of events in China. But sometimes he was more active than at other times. He never admitted he was wrong about any of his major changes, of course. The Hundred Flowers campaign had failed, he said, because the intellectuals had failed him. The Great Leap had nearly resulted in disaster because the people were not ready.

In any case, struggle itself could be more important than actual results, he thought. Yet there was no getting around the fact that he had now developed a record in many areas that to many people, including many people high in the CCP, smelled of failure.

It is not known whether it was because he was sick, weary, and fed up, or because he was pressured by others in the party, but before 1959 was over he had begun to let others take center stage. Keeping, of course, his position in the CCP, he gave up his position as head of state. His old Long March comrade, Liu Shaoqi, who had so often expressed displeasure with the policy turnings Mao had instigated in recent years, became China's president. Although Mao retained the most powerful position, the chairmanship of the party, increasingly more real power was in Liu's hands.

Liu was a superb organizer. In the old days he had specialized in underground organization. Now he believed that it was the economic development of the nation that should come first. This was very different from Mao's philosophy of constant struggle and his idea that changing the very nature of the Chinese people was more important than any immediate material benefits.

Often in the past, when pressure had built up in Peking, Mao would retreat to the countryside to think, write, and regain his energy. He now began spending longer periods of time away from Peking. Often these trips were to his home province, Hunan. There was talk that he no longer enjoyed the physical vigor needed to run a nation.

Mao by this time was not a well man. Periodically he would swim in one of China's great rivers to prove he still had his energy, making sure there were photographers around to publicize the event. But it is believed now that by the 1950s he already had Parkinson's disease, a progressive ailment that causes trembling and loss of coordination. It can be controlled, even for long periods, but as yet there is no cure.

Whatever the state of his health, Mao did not totally remove himself from government affairs. He was influential in pushing the careers of some officials, among them that of Hua Guofeng, a young politician who was working hard on development projects in Hunan and who would one day become premier and vice-chairman of the CCP.

Mao was also influential in aborting the careers of some of the officials who did not share his views. In particular, he went after Peng Dehuai, an old Red Army commander who had been in charge of the PLA forces in Korea and was now China's defense minister. Peng, always bold in expressing disagreements, had opposed the Great Leap and was saying the commune system had been set up too soon.

Mao was worried that Peng might go off on his own, followed by the PLA, and set up a power center in China that would rival that of the CCP. Working behind the scenes, Mao arranged for Peng's ouster, having him replaced with another strong Red Army veteran commander. Lin Biao—who before long would stand precariously on center stage himself—became the new defense minister.

And so Mao was not totally exiled from power. He continued to make certain his views were considered in party councils. He continued to decry the Americans, and particularly the Russians. But mostly he bided his time. Until the mid-sixties he made no major attempts to alter China's course.

That course was largely being determined by the loss of Russian aid and a series of crop failures. The people in Peking were attacking practical problems such as had not yet confronted the Communist state. Just as the Russians withdrew, a major drought began and lasted two years. Mao saw, to his great satisfaction, that it was only through the new systems of food distribution permitted by the communal use of land that famine was averted.

But the day-to-day administration was now in the hands of men who were diametrically opposed to what Mao had stood for in recent years. Ideology was not their main concern; they were interested in practical solutions to immediate problems. The term pragmatic was applied to those who followed this action, and these pragmatists were exemplified by a rising, outspoken, short, bullet-headed official from Szechuan, Deng Xiaoping, who had become the CCP's secretary general. Deng was reputed to have said in criticism of the Great Leap, "A donkey is certainly slow, but at least it rarely has an accident."

THE CULTURAL REVOLUTION

6

Nobody knows for sure how much influence Mao had between his retreat at the start of the 1960s and his tumultuous return in the second half of the decade. Although he spent more time than usual away from Peking, he was never a complete recluse. He concerned himself with power as well as with ideology, for it was his man, Lin Biao, who was directly in charge of the omnipresent PLA. Although Mao was not powerless, and despite whatever may have been going on beneath the surface, it was, nevertheless, the pragmatists, particularly Liu Shaoqi and Deng Xiaoping, who were setting the overall tone in China.

With pride, the Chinese completed, on their own, all the building programs that had been started with the help of the now departed Russian technicians. In the rural areas, the people, after getting through the bad harvests of the early 1960s without disaster, were producing more food than China had produced in the relatively bountiful years of the previous decade. Virtually all of the farm workers continued to live on communes as they do today. But now they lived in their own houses and worked nearby, as even greater emphasis was placed on the smaller production units.

During the Great Leap period, Mao had ordered that all village markets be done away with. No private sales of farm produce were allowed. But now the pragmatists decreed that the village markets be opened again, and allowed to operate the way they would in a non-Communist nation. The great bulk of China's food still came from communal farming, and was distributed equally to everyone. But peasants were again permitted to own private plots on which to grow their own crops, and sell them for whatever the market would bear.

Under the direction of the pragmatists, industrial production rose. Factory managers were given wide authority. The work methods they adopted did not have to fit any ideological interpretation as long as they were effective. The managers were allowed to pay more to the productive workers. Later Mao and Lin would complain that during this period factory managers began acting like the old factory owners in the days before the Communists governed.

In foreign affairs China was once more showing, as it had shown during the Korean War, that it was a power to be taken seriously. In the autumn of 1962 a border dispute with India broke out along the frontiers of Tibet. It was an old dispute, going back to the days of the Manchurian Empire in China and British rule in India. The Communists were determined to demonstrate that as the legitimate rulers of China, they would press traditional territorial claims.

The Indians attempted a quick military occupation of the mountainous area that was in dispute. Units of the PLA just as quickly drove them out. The Indians were chased into territory on the edge of the mountains that was actually inside India. Having humiliated the Indian army, the Chinese then withdrew behind what they considered the legitimate border.

In 1964 the world received further, chilling evidence that no one could toy with China. That year the Chinese set off their first nuclear device. This event was especially significant to the Chinese because for years before the split with the Soviet Union they had been asking the Russians to supply them with nuclear weapons; they had been refused any help connected with nuclear technology. The Russians thought

China could not become a nuclear power on its own, but now they were proved wrong.

During this time there were no sudden shifts in policy, nothing comparable to the Great Leap's romantic assumption that industrialization could be based on sheer will. Rather than attempt to speed up the process of creating an ideal Communist society, the pragmatists were becoming more lenient, emphasizing results over "correct thinking." There was no intellectual upheaval comparable to what had gone on during Mao's Hundred Flowers period.

Sitting on the sidelines, Mao seemed happy—at least to a degree—with what had happened so far to his country. Communism in China had gone through most of the stages he had foreseen. There had been the successful political and military revolution that had brought the CCP to power. Then the capitalist economy and the old landowner system had been replaced, and the system changed to the point where China's private sector was infinitesimal. On the whole Mao was happy with what had taken place, despite his immediate annoyance with Liu, Deng, and the other pragmatists in power for allowing some capitalist ways to creep back in.

But there was more to Mao's growing discontent than annoyance with new specific policy measures. Most of all he felt that the Chinese people were ready now for another stage in the development of Communism. They had done most of the things he had wanted them to do, but he still did not trust their overall attitude toward life. What they really wanted and what they were really thinking, he believed, were not very different from the desires and thoughts of their ancestors.

Again, actions were not enough for Mao. It was whether people were sincere in their actions that concerned him most. And because he did not think his people were sincere, he decided it was time for a new revolution in which the Chinese would finally break totally with the past, a revolution to change the way the people thought.

EARLY MOVES
BEHIND THE SCENES
As was shown by the way he had instigated the ouster of Peng Dehuai and the installation of Lin Biao in the defense ministry, Mao had never been ready to leave everything in the pragmatists' hands. Maybe for the moment he was sitting back and watching most of the time while the nation moved ahead without regard for his ideas concerning constant struggle and change. But no high official in China would make any move without calculating how or whether Mao would react to it. He had worked out the ideology to which even the most conservative pragmatists had to pay lip service at the very least. He had been the guiding force behind the military since the days it had operated like an outlaw band in the hills. No man in China was so venerated as Mao. There had probably never been a time in Chinese history when any one leader, not even the strongest of emperors, had enjoyed comparable prestige.

Liu and Deng might for the moment appear to be the guiding forces in China. The suave Chou En-lai might be China's most effective spokesman abroad. But no one in the top echelons could afford to forget for a moment that Mao was still the chairman of the CCP and more than any other individual, commanded the loyalty of the army and of the peasants.

Yet Mao came to feel he had been forgotten. He grumbled about factory managers who had forgotten ideology, about rural medical workers who he claimed were gravitating to an easier life in the cities, about peasants who were becoming small-time capitalists. And, as he grumbled, he knew whom to blame. Later he would write of how during this time the pragmatists "treated me like a dead ancestor."

In some ways it did seem as if Mao were a man forgotten by time. The best-selling book in China in the first half of the 1960s was not anything Chairman Mao had written but rather a volume called *How to Be a Good Communist;* it had been written by President Liu. Visitors who saw Mao in 1964 and 1965 noted that nurses were often in attendance. The trembling that goes with Parkinson's had gotten worse. Some of these visitors came away saying he was no longer part of China's future. But they were forgetting the very real power that he still held.

Mao was doing much more than reading and studying in these years. One result of his close collaboration with Lin Biao, who headed the PLA, was Lin's announcement that the army would become a "great school for Mao Zedong's Thought." Throughout the country choirs made up of PLA members sang Mao's words set to music. The PLA's official newspaper, the *Liberation Army Daily*, each day featured quotes from the chairman.

Mao's writings also appeared in a book that was soon selling far more than anything written by Liu. In fact, during the second half of the 1960s, far more copies of this book were sold than any other book published anywhere in the world. This was the small volume, entitled *Quotations from Chairman Mao*, which would become known simply as the "Little Red Book." It contained short quotes from Mao's writings, giving his views on all manner of subjects. It was first published by the PLA, and Lin made sure that everyone in the army had a copy. Editions issued after 1965 carried an introduction by Lin which began, "Comrade Mao Zedong is the greatest Marxist-Leninist in our era."

Mao was also making his influence felt beyond the PLA. He was the prime mover behind a program called the "Socialist Education Movement." It was designed to make young people, who had no memory of the years of fighting from the hills and the civil war, think along more radical lines. The movement had no apparent support from the men ruling in Peking, and yet it caught on throughout the country, especially in the rural areas. The pragmatists resisted the program, but it was impossible in Communist China to put a stop to anything called "Socialist Education."

In study groups of the Socialist Education Program, the young people were led by supporters of Mao and stirred up to oppose whatever did not fit with Mao's Thought. Liu and Deng had rehabilitated many of the intellectuals who had been sent away in disgrace in the 1950s, but now the young people were taught to oppose these intellectuals. The movement did not immediately affect the position of the pragmatists, but it helped to set the stage for what would come. While Mao seemed to be staying in the background, his support in the army, his support among rural youth, and his overall prestige were on the rise.

Another sign that Mao's influence was waxing was the state of the nation's cultural life. His wife, Chiang Ching, the former Shanghai actress, had drawn close to Lin. Under her direction and patronage—with the approval of the defense minister—soldiers, along with professional performers, began putting on elaborate propaganda dramas that combined singing and dancing. These shows were replacing the traditional performing arts throughout China.

The theme of all these productions was class struggle. When people went out for a night of entertainment, they were presented with lavish dance-dramas that exalted not the pragmatists in Peking but the Thought of Mao.

MAO'S RETURN
In the autumn of 1965, Mao and Chiang Ching left for Shanghai and began to rally the chairman's supporters. For six months they divided their time between quarters in what had once been a private French club and a villa at a nearby lake resort. It was the longest period of time Mao had spent out-

side Peking since before his triumphal entry in 1949. But it did not mean he had decided to bow out.

A literary battle was the first rumbling of what was about to come. On November 10 a Shanghai cultural publication carried a strong piece of criticism of a play, called *Hai Rui Dismissed from Office*, that had been written and produced by the deputy mayor of Peking, Wu Han. The play was a historical piece about an emperor who had unfairly sent away a loyal official. It was clear to the more knowledgeable who watched it that the play was really about Mao's dismissal of his loyal old troop commander and defense minister, Peng.

The play was not an isolated attack on Mao. While Mao had been away from the center of power, various articles and stories had appeared that were meant to criticize him, though his name was never mentioned. He had been compared to a mediocre, aging athlete, and even to a man who suffers a loss of memory and is headed for insanity. But now Mao felt strong enough to strike back. Before long, newspapers all over the country had taken up the attack on Wu Han's *Hai Rui Dismissed from Office*.

The next big event signaling Mao's comeback was even more bizarre than conducting politics through theater criticism. In the middle of 1966, after many more months with no public appearances and amid rumors he was dead, Mao suddenly turned up in the city of Wuhan with newsmen, photographers, and television cameramen in tow. As he had done in the past, but with far more hoopla, he was ready to prove his prowess by going swimming.

He plunged into the Yangtze River. According to the controlled media's news reports, he swam over 9 miles (15 km) in 65 minutes despite treacherous currents, and walked out of the water looking relaxed, vigorous, and refreshed. He looked, in other words, like a man ready for, and capable of, intense action.

In the preceding months he had been talking about struggle again. He had spoken about struggle with enemies both internal and external. An important element of the climate in China now was that many Chinese felt they were threatened from abroad, just as they had been in 1950. And this threat became another matter on which Mao and the pragmatists fell out.

The source of this external threat was in neighboring South Vietnam where America had been building up its presence. When the French withdrew from Vietnam in 1954, the Communist Vietnamese guerrillas who had fought them had quickly taken over the northern part of the country. In the south, however, a pro-Western government had been installed with the blessing of France and America. At the peace conference in Geneva, where Chou had helped work out the settlements it had been agreed that elections would be held to unite the country under one government. Both sides knew that the Communists would win such elections since they were the heroes of the fight against the French.

Faced with this circumstance, the United States backed off from its commitment to free elections in Vietnam. The Americans proceeded to shore up the South Vietnamese government, at first with a handful of military advisers, but eventually with actual combat troops. But no matter what America did, the Communists from the north continued to gain ground in the south. By 1966 America had a half-million men in South Vietnam. The Chinese felt very much the way Americans would have felt if there were a half-million anti-American troops fighting in Mexico. And in Washington some military men were saying openly that the way to win the war was to push into China, a major source of supplies for North Vietnam.

In response, the leaders in Peking were now talking about sending a joint Chinese-Russian troop contingent to Vietnam. Mao, on the other hand, stuck to the view of world revolution he had worked out long before. While China might

send supplies to Vietnam, he said, the war would be won by the Vietnamese Communists themselves, fighting the kind of guerrilla actions that Mao had found so successful.

An indication of how opposed to the pragmatists Mao was on this issue came when the leader of the Japanese Communist Party arrived in China for talks about Vietnam. At this meeting Mao lost all patience, just as he had in the mid-1940s when talking to Americans who wanted to bring him closer to Chiang. When it was proposed to send troops to Indochina, rather than encouraging a Maoist guerrilla war, Mao shouted at the men who were officially in charge of his country: "You weak-kneed people in Peking!"

THE RAMPAGE BEGINS

Bv the autumn of 1966 wall posters containing Mao's latest thoughts on all manner of subjects were going up all over China. Through these posters, he was calling on the people to engage in what was virtually a second civil war. He labeled this new revolt the "Great Proletarian Cultural Revolution." The idea behind it was to return to the true way—Mao's way—of Chinese Communism.

He planned now to bring about the kind of agreement that he had expected, and failed to get, in his Hundred Flowers campaign. This meant his revolution would not be based on, in fact would oppose, the country's intellectuals. Mao now

At the beginning of the Cultural Revolution in October 1966, Mao attended a rally celebrating China's National Day. Defense Minister Lin Biao stands between Mao and Premier Chou En-lai.

felt that the educated people in China were supporters more of the old ways than the new ways brought by the Communist Revolution. He said the results of the revolt would be more dramatic than those he had expected from the Great Leap. Since he blamed the failure of the Great Leap on government and party officials, they too would be targets of the new revolution.

He spoke mainly to the country's youth, to the 300 million Chinese who had been too young to experience the first revolution. Young people from throughout the country were organized, fed, and transported to all the important cities by the PLA, led by Lin. These youths, most of them teenagers, were officially designated as "Red Guards," and given khaki military uniforms with Red Guard armbands. Mao assured the Red Guards that, "To rebel is justified." He told them they had a license to "Knock down the old." Before the autumn was over they were on a rampage all over the country.

Wherever they went they carried copies of the Little Red Book, waving it as if it offered almost religious sanction to their activities. They lashed out at even the smallest matters that they felt did not fit Mao's Thought. They attacked people wearing sunglasses, which they considered a middle-class affectation. People who played chess were considered fair game because chess was considered too Russian. Almost anything anyone did was enough to have him or her labeled a revisionist, meaning someone opposed to the traditional interpretation of Communism. The Guards ransacked homes containing books because intellectuals were suspect, and they looted from anyone who looked too well off to be a true Communist. They smashed the temples of China's old philosophical religions, Buddhism, Taoism and Confucianism. They even tore up the graves of dead men suspected of being revisionists.

Often the Red Guards' attacks were cruel, as when a throng broke into the home of Peking's mayor, Peng Zhen, late at night. They rushed into his bedroom, turned on the light, and ordered him to come with them to be criticized in public. "Peng Zhen's face turned ashen out of surprise and he could not even dress himself," one Guard wrote with glee.

It was common to parade their victims before hooting mobs. Suspected revisionists were forced to wear dunce caps—a peculiar adaptation from the West—while they made mandatory confessions of their supposed errors.

Mao asked his old comrade Chu Teh, now in retirement, the Red Army commander who had been part of the Chu-Mao legend, to speak out in support of the Cultural Revolution. He even asked Chu to confess errors in his thinking. When this national hero refused, he was denounced in public as a "big warlord and careerist who wormed his way into the Party."

Wall posters were placed on every vacant space—not just on walls, but also on trees, on statues, even on side-walks. They continued to carry revolutionary quotations from Mao, and attacks on officials, and often they even denounced various Red Guard factions too.

Mao continued to tell the Red Guards that they had the future in their hands. It was up to them, he said, to snatch power from the revisionist officials. Late in 1966, in a series of ten sunrise rallies in Peking, he personally greeted eleven million of the teenage zealots. At such rallies the Guards would wave their Little Red Books and Defense Minister Lin would exhort them to continue ferreting out revisionists and smashing any objects that smacked of the past. Mao himself remained aloof. He would stand high above the throng, his radical wife beside him, both of them wearing PLA fatigues with red stars on their caps. He would raise an arm, as if in benediction. He remained silent, but his mere appearance was enough to make the teenagers leap up and down, and shout and weep. It was the cult of personality carried to its furthest extreme. It was almost as if Mao had become a diety.

Everywhere in China now people of all ages were wearing badges that carried Mao's effigy.

Many reasons have since been given for Mao's behavior at this time. One suggestion is that at the age of seventy-three, in failing health, he simply lacked the energy to restrain the forces he had unleashed. Another is that Lin Biao, who was personally ambitious, was pushing Mao, expecting one day to inherit his mantle. Also, it is possible that at this moment, despite what he said before and later, he had come to believe that a cult of personality was needed if the people of a backward country were to be rallied to improve themselves.

Whatever the reasons for his behavior, he seemed at this point very different from the man he had been. In the past he had spent long hours writing poems and books. Now all he was writing was a batch of wall-poster slogans to excite the mobs. In the past he had always said it was important that students learn to think for themselves, confident that they would eventually come to believe sincerely in what he himself believed. Now he was promoting blind faith as the route to accepting his ideas.

When Liu, who had worked closely with Mao for most of the past forty-five years, and Deng tried to limit the Red Guards' excesses, Mao lashed out at them the way he had lashed out at Chu. He accused them of being similar to old warlords, and said they had no place in Communist China.

By the start of 1967, with no public sign from Mao yet that he felt restraint was needed, the country was in such chaos that it had come to a standstill. Not only were all the schools and universities closed, normal daily work had been interrupted everywhere in China, sometimes because of the turmoil and sometimes just because the workers wanted to see the excitement.

But although tens of thousands of people lost their lives as the Guards ran wild and although Mao was not yet ready

In a scene typical of the mass rallies of the
Cultural Revolution, this crowd gathers around
a large picture of Chairman Mao in Shansi Province,
where Red Guards had just seized power from
the ruling Communist Party committee.

to curb the teenagers, he had not, after all, abandoned reason. Liu and Deng were stripped of their jobs, but they were still living, if under house arrest, at their homes in the Forbidden City. Moreover, it is generally believed now that all through this period Mao was, from time to time, speaking with them.

There is no good evidence that Mao ever really meant to turn his country completely over to the Red Guards. To Mao, it seems clear in retrospect, the Cultural Revolution, though more extreme, was at the end nothing more nor less than his other drastic policy changes. It was another attempt to stir up the country so that the Chinese would not become complacent. It was a policy meant to prevail for only a limited time, intended to keep the people on the road to achieving Mao's version of Communism. Again he had fallen back on the peasantry—young people brought in from the countryside to purify the cities.

RESTRAINING THE RED GUARDS

It was still early in 1967 that Mao began easing off his attacks on the so-called revisionists of the older generations. He began the first tentative moves to curb what were now being referred to openly in Mao's own circles as the "little devils" who made up the Red Guards.

A turning point came in February when the Red Guards seized government offices in Shanghai and announced they were forming a new government there to be known as the "Shanghai Commune." Mao summoned a pair of journalists who had been at the forefront of the Cultural Revolution in Shanghai. He warned them that the city, and possibly the whole country, was sinking into chaos, that soon there would be no effective government at all. The journalists spread the word, and the Shanghai Commune came to an end. So effective was Mao's power that a few words spoken to journalists were enough to turn Shanghai around.

By now the Red Guards, who had begun at the outset to

split into factions, had become so faction-ridden that they were spending more time attacking each other than attacking their revisionist enemies. At one point, there were 1417 distinct and separate Red Guard groups in only three provinces and three large cities. Mao began traveling around the country to see the situation for himself. He found that not only were the Red Guards fighting each other, they were also coming into conflict with city workers, and many members of the army were turning against them.

Word reached him that in Wuhan the Red Guards had become especially unpopular. He sent two envoys to Wuhan, and they were promptly taken into custody by the local PLA commander. Chou En-lai rushed to Wuhan and talked the commander into releasing Mao's representatives. But the military had made its point. Mao came to accept the fact that, as anarchy increased and more people felt in danger, the military was turning against the Cultural Revolution and was becoming far more popular than the Red Guards.

Before 1967 was over virtually every official of any prominence at all, with the exception of Mao himself, had been denounced by the Red Guards. Even Chou, who was relatively moderate but had always followed Mao even in his wildest policy turnings, was held prisoner briefly. He was reviled as the "rotten boss of the bourgeoisie." One Red Guard faction wanted to put Chou on trial. Mao, it was said, told the Guards they could try Chou if they put him on trial as well.

He also expressed his disapproval when the Red Guards burned the British embassy. By the summer of 1967 he was talking much more of unity than of revolution. When he left Peking to travel around the country again, it was Chou, who was now disliked by all Red Guard factions, who remained to preside over the still raging Cultural Revolution. Mao began talking occasionally like a moderate. "You cannot be skeptical about everything," he told the Guards; "you cannot overthrow everything." By late in the year, even though he was still speaking more of revolution than of moderation, he ordered the Red Guards to go home and go back to school. "Can the Red Guards assume command?" he asked. "They will certainly be toppled tomorrow after being installed today. This is because they are politically immature . . . The Red Guards are incompetent."

Mao next called in the army to restore order, just as at first he had called in the army to build up and aid the Red Guards. PLA members were soon seen taking charge on communes, in factories, in schools, and at local government headquarters. Mao explained this sudden shift by saying, "Soldiers are just workers and peasants wearing uniforms." But they were really much more. In 1968 there was a new form of organization called the "Revolutionary Committee" running just about every enterprise in China. A Revolutionary Committee included PLA members, Red Guards, and party officials. The remaining Red Guards were officially part of the power structure, but in practice it was the PLA, and to a lesser extent the CCP, that was in charge. The Red Guards' power had been ended. The country was being run mainly by the military.

In official words coming out of Peking, the Great Proletarian Cultural Revolution lasted past the mid-1970s. But what most people think of as the Cultural Revolution—the chaos, the teenage rampages—was over by 1969. And when it was over it turned out that China had not been changed any more drastically than it had been by Mao's other radical turnings. No lasting reorganization of society resulted from the Cultural Revolution. There had been shifts in personnel, but there was no entirely new order of leaders running the country.

What had happened was simply that Mao had emerged for everyone to see as the number one man in China again. The peasants had always believed he was nothing less than the embodiment of the Communist state. Now everyone in China knew his strength. In terms of pure power, he was clearly the paramount ruler.

BEYOND THE CULTURAL REVOLUTION

7

Until the end Mao remained consistent in his seeming inconsistency. For the rest of the ten-year period that started with the Cultural Revolution in 1966, and concluded with Mao's death in 1976, he remained at the helm, steering first this way and then that way. For periods the forces of moderation, stability, and economic progress would seem to be in control. But at other times it would be the advocates of constant change, constant struggle, constant revolution.

In April of 1969 the first CCP congress since 1958 was convened. The deliberations, held in great secrecy, lasted for three weeks, which was longer than usual and indicated there was considerable debate. At the end it was stated that this meeting had brought the Cultural Revolution to its successful culmination.

The congress confirmed Mao's supremacy in China. A new constitution was put into effect stating that the "Thought of Mao Zedong" was again the official ideology of the party. Liu Shaoqi, was formally stripped of all his offices and expelled from party membership, final confirmation that he and other pragmatists were out of public life. Lin Biao was exalted as Mao's "close comrade in arms," and it seemed clear that as vice-chairman of the CCP, the defense minister would be Mao's successor.

It seemed that the CCP would be dominated by men who were loyal to Mao and supported Mao's Thought. Almost 40 percent of the members elected to the CCP's Central Committee were from Mao's home province of Hunan and Lin's of Hupei, although the two provinces hold less than 11 percent of China's people.

Although the congress apparently reconfirmed the new power of the army, which had just been used to control the Red Guards, there were indications that more radical elements would be predominant in party affairs. Mao's wife was elected to the Politburo and so were two of her close associates from Shanghai, the center of radical intrigue. Chiang Ching and these two, Yao Wenyuan, a prominent theorist, and Zhang Chunqiao, who would rise to deputy premier, had been Mao's most trusted associates while the Red Guards were being spurred on to their excesses.

The makeup of the Politburo also seemed to confirm Lin's power. Another new member was Lin's young second wife, Ye Chun, who served as his personal chief of staff.

In some ways the new power structure confirmed by the congress made it anyone's guess what direction China would take. On the one hand, the radicals had more important positions than ever. On the other hand, nearly half of the delegates to the congress were dressed in PLA uniforms.

One of Mao's favorite dicta was that "Power grows from the barrel of a gun," but he always added that "the Party must always control the gun." In the past, although he had created the PLA and used it to his own ends, he had been as leery of a military take-over as of any other possible factional challenge to his authority.

One reason it was so hard to tell from the congress which way Mao was now moving was the position of Lin. The defense minister seemed clearly the number two man in the country now. He had risen to such heights because during the

Cultural Revolution the most fervent rampaging Maoists had helped lift him up. Yet there were vast differences between Lin, the professional soldier, and those who had helped him to his current position.

THE FALL OF LIN
Looking back, it is easy to see how Mao and Lin would come into conflict. During and after the Cultural Revolution the army had a much greater role in government than it had had before. Mao, as a student of history, knew how hard it is to get soldiers who have tasted political power to return to the barracks.

And, probably more important, Mao and Lin had basic differences in their approach to getting about the job of building and governing China. In the past Lin had often spoken of the need for "absolute authority" in the affairs of the country. This was, of course, very different from Mao's concept of constant change, from Mao's sharp veerings, of course. Lin's views contrasted sharply with Mao's willingness from time to time to unleash against constituted authority any forces and factions if he thought such acts would contribute to the struggle that would lead to his goals.

Furthermore, as it soon became clear, Mao never fully trusted Lin. He suspected his defense minister was flattering him for purposes of self-advancement. Actually, as early as 1966 Mao had written to his wife about how Lin was promoting the Little Red Book: "I have never believed that those little books of mine could have such fantastic magic," Mao said, "yet he [Lin] blew them up, and the whole country followed." Mao may have promoted the cult of personality at the height of the Cultural Revolution, but he was suspicious that Lin was promoting the personality cult because Lin himself hoped to be the beneficiary.

Lin kept urging Mao to take over the position of head of state, which had been vacant since the fall of Liu. Mao thought that perhaps Lin wanted the position reinstated either because he expected to get it himself right away or because he wanted it there for the taking when Mao died. So Mao decided China would not have an official head of state. The party chairman, hence, would more clearly than ever be the country's most powerful official.

There were also tensions coming from China's changing foreign policy objectives. Many PLA officers, and it is now believed Lin continued to be one of them, still saw America, not Russia, as China's main threat. But Mao, who for years now had emphasized that Russia and America were both threats to China, was coming to the view that the American threat was waning. The Americans had not backed Chiang Kai-shek in an attack on the mainland after all, and by 1969 they seemed to realize that their intervention in Vietnam had been a mistake.

Russia, meanwhile, was getting harsher. The Russians in 1968 sent tanks to put down opposition led by fellow Communists in Czechoslovakia. The Chinese Communists were as far apart in ideology from the Russians as were the Czechs. Was it not possible, Mao asked, that one day the Russians would send their tanks into China? For a few weeks just before the 1969 CCP congress there had actually been fighting, intense if inconclusive, between Russian and Chinese troops in a disputed border region at the Amur and Ussuri rivers in China's northeast. Nearly a thousand men, most of them Chinese, had been killed.

By late August, and early September of 1970, however, it was Mao's differences with Lin, not the Russians, which came out at a meeting of the CCP's Central Committee of Lushan, a mountain resort in Kiangsi. The question of a head of state that had been raised at the last party congress came up again. Lin and his backers now proposed that a president with sweeping powers be named. They also pushed the theory, long opposed by Mao, that history was influenced by the occasional appearance of a rare genius—renewing all Mao's suspicions about Liu's motives in promoting the Mao cult. Now Mao attacked the rare genius theory directly in a speech to the Central Committee. He went so far as to say the theory came originally from the disgraced former president, Liu. The Central Committee dropped the plan to re-create a presidency, vacant since Liu's fall. Now Mao's and Lin's differences were out in the open. It no longer looked certain that Lin would be the successor.

It is possible that by now Lin feared he would be fired from his post as defense minister. Mao, after all, was on record as opposing him on the rare genius theory, the need for a head of state, the American question, and also the central role the PLA was playing. The radicals who supported Lin now began to drift away from him, and he was left only with PLA officers, albeit some in key positions, as his vocal supporters.

Mao began to undermine what support was left for Lin. Although the military establishment in Peking had become much like conventional military establishments in other nations, out in the provinces there were commanders, many of whom had been on the Long March as young men, who were totally loyal to Mao. They believed that the PLA, operating amidst the people, should be like no other military establishment on earth. During the winter and spring of 1971 Mao traveled about the country, dropping in on command headquarters, telling commanders of how he no longer supported Lin. And back in the capital, in a move orchestrated by Chou En-lai, key Lin supporters were dismissed from Lin's base, the Peking Military Command.

For years wall posters had carried Mao's slogan, "Let the people of the whole country learn from the PLA." At this time a new wall-poster slogan appeared: "Let the PLA learn from the people of the whole country."

It now seems clear that when it became obvious that

Mao was plotting against his defense minister, Lin and his supporters began to put together a counterplot. The final, violent outcome was not announced until the following year. What had happened, the people were told, was that on September 12, 1971, Lin and five supporters from the Politburo were killed when an aircraft they were using to flee to the Soviet Union ran out of fuel and crashed in the Soviet-bloc country of Outer Mongolia.

There is still no definitive version of the story. It is known, however, that Lin had used his army base to build a more serious challenge to Mao than anyone had before. Mao had felt so insecure that in the week before the plane crash he had changed his residence at least twice. It was said that a house he used in Shanghai was strafed by fighter planes. Other stories put out by the government include one stating that poison was put in food intended for Mao, and another that claimed an army officer had raised a gun to shoot Mao but changed his mind at the last minute. Still another government story said that there were plans to blow up a train on which Mao was traveling. Whatever the details, few observers now doubt that Lin was actually planning a coup d'etat. One official story had it that the plotters were betrayed at the last minute by a patriotic daughter born to Lin by his first wife.

Whether Lin was really killed by accident while trying to escape, or whether he was murdered, possibly well before the plane crash, will probably never be known for certain. The Russians who inspected the wreckage said the bodies aboard were burned beyond recognition. But most Chinese believe Lin came close to overthrowing the Great Helmsman.

THE AMERICAN CARD
At the same time that Mao and Lin were falling out, then plotting against each other, Mao was making steady progress with his new plan to draw China closer to America. In the

years to come there would be a great deal of talk by American politicians and journalists about how America was getting the upper hand against the Russians by "playing the China card." But it can as easily, or perhaps more easily, be looked at another way. By the time Lin was killed, Mao was besting the Soviets by playing the American card.

The time was ripe. In America, President Lyndon Johnson had been forced into retirement because of opposition to the war he led in Vietnam. The man who won America's 1968 presidential election, Richard Nixon, had once been one of the most vocal foreign supporters of Chiang Kai-shek. Nixon, however, was unwilling to stop the war despite his promises in the election campaign, and he soon found it increasingly difficult to face American antiwar sentiment. From the American viewpoint, it was clear that virtually no one still believed the fiction that China belonged to Chiang Kai-shek. In fact, China was clearly the most important Communist country in Asia, and Nixon apparently felt that without support from the most powerful of Asia's Communists he would never get America out of Vietnam. Moreover, since the polls were showing that his administration was unpopular, he apparently concluded he needed a dramatic new diplomatic triumph to convince the voters he deserved a second term in office.

So this old supporter of Chiang began making overtures to Mao. In 1970 Nixon ended the ban on American trade with China, and announced that henceforth Americans would be free to travel to China whenever they wanted.

In the spring of 1971 the Chinese made their first response. It came over a seemingly trivial matter, but it was their first open act of friendship to America since the founding of the Communist state. They issued an invitation to an American Ping-Pong team, playing at the world championships in Japan, to visit Peking.

In the summer, Nixon sent his foreign policy chief, Henry Kissinger, on a secret mission to confer with Mao, Chou, and other officials in Peking—the first trip of a government official between the two countries in the People's Republic's history. With the way paved, Nixon himself arrived in Peking for an eight-day visit in February of 1972. At this point no American president had ever stayed as long as eight days in any foreign country. It was also the first time an American president engaged in negotiations in a country with which America did not have diplomatic relations.

Nixon's mere presence in China was a triumph for Mao. It was more than an indication that China no longer had to worry about an American attack. Perhaps most important, the world saw not only that America was seeking peace with China, but that it was the Americans going to the Chinese, not the other way around.

And Mao won specific concessions from America. The United States for the first time took the view that it "does not challenge" the claim that Taiwan belongs to China, and that it hopes for "a personal settlement of the Taiwan question by the Chinese themselves." Although formal recognition was left to the future, for practical purposes the Americans now recognized the government in Peking, not that on Taiwan, as the legitimate government of China. There would be cultural and trade exchanges between the two nations. Diplomatic offices, though not official embassies, would be set up by the Chinese in Washington and the Americans in Peking.

With America no longer clinging to Chiang, the world got the message. Even before the Nixon visit, Communists from Peking had taken over from the Nationalists as China's representatives in the United Nations.

THE STRUGGLE GOES ON
Any of a number of events that took place in the early 1970s in China might have seemed to unsophisticated Western observers to constitute the end of the story of Mao's struggles. He had defeated Lin; he had defeated the pro-Russian

elements in Peking; he had at last gained the recognition that the People's Republic had sought in the world. But Mao, though he turned eighty in 1973, was in many ways the same man he had always been. It is perhaps more than symbolic that, unlike most active men when they age, no new character lines appeared on his face.

The course he steered was no more a fixed course than it had ever been. Mao still believed in a world in flux and he was still an advocate of constant struggle. Until the very end, he kept China on a zigzagging path. Sometimes he would steer the course desired by the pragmatists. Sometimes he would follow the plans of the radicals who had waged the Cultural Revolution.

The fortunes of other Chinese leaders continued to change rapidly. During the period in which Lin was defeated and China reached an accord with America, Chou En-lai, the only major leader to survive all of Mao's turnings, appeared to be nearly Mao's equal. The forces of moderation seemed to be triumphing. Efforts were made to stress academic subjects over ideological indoctrination in the schools, which had severely lowered their academic standards in the years after the Cultural Revolution excesses. Also, there was now less regimentation in the communes, and material rewards were being offered again as incentives to workers in factories. It seemed almost as great a swing to the right as the swing that had occurred after the Great Leap. Mao made one of his rare personal appearances at the funeral of a former foreign minister, Chen Yi. The appearance was significant because Chen Yi had been one of the officials purged in the Cultural Revolution.

For the time people were speaking more freely. There were still pro-Lin pockets in the military and sometimes pro-Lin statements were getting into print. Near Canton the daughter who was supposed to have betrayed Lin was shot, apparently by soldiers, and a strip of cloth bearing the inscription TREASON AND HEINOUS CRIME was pinned to her body. But Mao was conciliatory in his dealings with the military. He continued gradually to switch commanders' postings so that those loyal to him would hold the key positions, but there were no mass purges of PLA men. Mao and Chou received a continuing stream of heads of foreign states, who now journeyed to Peking in the wake of Nixon. At the UN, China went about its business, observing all diplomatic niceties, and quickly emerged as the leading spokesman for the Third World.

At one diplomatic reception in Peking the guests noticed to their astonishment that among their number was Deng Xiaoping. This man who stood for everything the Red Guards had fought against had been rehabilitated. He was now made a deputy premier.

But when the next CCP congress convened, in August of 1973, there were signs that Mao was again promoting the radicals. Lin's old job of vice-chairman of the CCP was divided among five men—Chou, who was seventy-five, three others in their late sixties or seventies, and one who, in Chinese government terms, was a mere boy of thirty-nine. This young man, Wang Hongwen, was a former textile worker who had emerged in the Cultural Revolution as a radical leader in Shanghai. Wang was given the honor of delivering one of the two main reports—the other being given by Chou—at the congress. Immediately there was talk that Wang, who had the strong support of Mao's radical wife, might be Mao's successor.

But, although in his remaining years Mao often boosted the leftists, Wang was not being treated like a future chairman. Unlike Lin in his glory years, Wang had no official designation indicating he was especially close to Mao personally, and he was rarely seen at Mao's side.

Still, the radicals had cause to be pleased with Mao. From early 1974 onward he led a new ideological campaign that was gratifying to the sort of people who had supported the Cultural Revolution. This was his anti-Confucius drive. Wall posters appeared again with slogans from the Cultural Revolution. These slogans were used as attacks on the thinking of the old sage who had laid out the rules concerning the kind of personal and family loyalties which the Chinese had followed for centuries. Many Communists had long sought to destroy the Confucian system of loyalties in favor of loyalty first and foremost to the Communist state.

In the schools and colleges, in the factories and on the communal farms, everyone was taught to hate Confucius. But it did not lead to the rampages of the previous decade. The anti-Confucius campaign could be interpreted in many different ways. To Mao's wife, Chiang Ching—still dominant in cultural life and still attacking classical culture—it meant an attack on everything that had gone on before the Cultural Revolution. To Chou En-lai, it meant an ideology with the useful purpose of uniting the forces, many of them moderate, that had brought about the fall of Lin and again consolidated Mao's power. To Mao himself it was probably nothing more than another device to keep the people off-guard, to remind them that Communism meant a constant struggle.

MAO'S FINAL TURNINGS

Mao, who was growing noticeably more feeble, continued to appear for photographers with visiting world leaders. These photo sessions were intended to show he was still active and still in charge. But increasingly, until his death in September of 1976, he seemed to be vacillating. Sometimes he would lash out at the radicals, particularly at his wife. Their marriage had soured, and after early 1973 Mao and Chiang Ching lived in separate houses. But Mao did not purge her from the party and she continued to speak out.

Deng Xiaoping, the leader of the pragmatists, sometimes seemed to be gaining the upper hand in his new role as deputy premier. When Chou En-lai died of cancer, in early 1976, there was wide speculation that Deng would be named premier. But Mao kept pragmatists and radicals alike off-balance. The acting premiership went to Hua Guofeng, an obscure official from Hunan whose career Mao had begun promoting during his years of retreat between the Great Leap and the Cultural Revolution.

Since Hua had followed Mao through all the turnings of the Cultural Revolution, he had often sounded like a radical. On the other hand, the radicals did not consider him one of their own. He had been equally willing to follow Mao when Mao had raised up the pragmatists again. It was widely believed Mao had already said Hua should be his successor, but Hua simply did not have the stature to be taken very seriously by either the radicals or the pragmatists.

starting early in 1976, the radicals had become more vocal than they had been for nearly a decade. With a steady stream of radical slogans appearing on wall posters in the style of the 1960s, it appeared almost as if the Cultural Revolution, which had never officially been ended, was being revived on a smaller scale.

After naming Hua acting premier, Mao turned on Deng, saying he had "never been a Marxist." A press campaign was launched against him. He was attacked as never having believed in Mao's ideology, and as being a "capitalist roader." Deng was again stripped of all official positions. But this time other members of the Politburo voluntarily left Peking with him as a show of support. Also, this time his supporters were strong enough so that he remained a member of the party.

Chou's death left the party split still between the radicals and the pragmatists. Mao, however, no longer appeared to have the strength to decide upon, and enforce, the CCP's direction. A sign of China's state of drift came when a spontaneous antigovernment riot broke out.

The occasion was the Spring Festival, a traditional Chinese holiday, commemorated since ancient times, on which the Chinese honor the dead. In Peking's great T'ien An Men Square, on the steps of the Monument to the People's Heroes, a vast number of wreaths and poems honoring Chou En-lai appeared overnight. Then vast crowds gathered in the square. Some of the poems went much further than commemorating Chou. They spoke of how China had lost its direction. A member of the crowd shouted, "What is the greatest problem at present? Where is China going? That is the biggest problem." Other poems criticized Mao for being high-handed in his rule, such as one saying, "China is no longer the China of yore. And the people are no longer wrapped in sheer ignorance." And others were more personal, such as one praising Mao's first wife, Yang Kaihui—the praise intended as a jab at the radical Chiang Ching.

The authorities had the wreaths and poems removed, and this touched off a riot. More than 100,000 people rioted in the disturbance that lasted fourteen hours. Vehicles were overturned and burned. Many people were badly injured, and a few were killed, before any attempt to restore order was made.

The Politburo was hastily called into session. Deng was officially dismissed from his jobs. Hua was given the full title of premier, and a new title as first vice-chairman of the CCP. And he was, finally, designated as Mao's heir. Members of a militia—not members of the regular army—were sent in to disperse the rioters.

These decisions were Mao's, but everyone knew his days were numbered. The leaders of the PLA, most of whom had venerated Chou, made it clear they were merely biding their time until Mao's death. The pragmatists had proved strong enough to keep Deng in the CCP. And now Deng, although officially in disgrace, was openly showing his contempt for Mao. At one point he said, "If they tell you that you're a capitalist roader it means you're doing a good job."

In any case it is doubtful that after April, Mao was well enough to be making any more decisions. Wall posters went up in Peking saying DEFEND CHAIRMAN MAO, an indication that he was no longer able to defend himself, or control events. Foreign visitors were still being brought to see him, but they said later that they often could not understand his words. In June, 1976, there was finally official confirmation of what everyone knew. A foreign ministry official made a momentous announcement: "Chairman Mao is well advanced in years and is still busy with his work. The Central Committee of our Party has decided not to arrange for [him] to meet foreign distinguished visitors."

It is not known if Mao joined in the decision. It is known that it was not made by the full Central Committee. The radicals, who always acted in Mao's name, wanted no announcement of his condition—and the news that he would no longer meet foreign leaders was news that his condition was very bad indeed. The pragmatists expected to take charge after his death, and hence pushed for the announcement, although they did not feel strong enough to move while he lived. For the moment, however, Chiang Ching seemed to have China in her hands. She controlled the telephone lines to Mao's quarters and also the now small trickle of visitors.

In the summer all of the Politburo members arrived at the chairman's bedside. "Help Chiang Ching," he started to say. There was disagreement later whether he finished the sentence with the words "to carry the Red Flag" or "to correct her errors."

In midsummer the old PLA commander Chu Teh died. And then there was a strange and disturbing happening. An earthquake leveled the city of Tangshan east of Peking. A quarter of a million people were killed. In Chinese folklore,

In Peking's T'ien An Men Square, mourners bow their heads before a portrait of Chairman Mao.

such a natural disaster signals the end of a dynasty. By late August, Mao, in his eighty-third year, was in a coma.

And then on September 12, 1976 the government radio carried the expected announcement: "Chairman Mao has left this world."

CHINA AFTER MAO

During the years since Mao's death, China has continued to prosper. It is, however, the pragmatists, led by Deng Xiaoping, who now hold power, not the radicals who followed Mao's revolutionary ideology and had long been protected by him. In the summer of 1981, the CCP Central Committee officially declared that Mao had been wrong in emphasizing constant struggle and wrong in starting the Cultural Revolution. Mao was praised for having made China free of foreign influence, leading the successful revolution against the Nationalists, and setting the nation on the road to Communism. But it was declared that in the future China would concentrate on practical matters, not on Maoist ideology.

Still, Mao Zedong casts a shadow over modern China such as no dead leader casts over any other major country in the world. He was the Marx, Lenin, and Stalin of the Chinese revolution. It was he who had led the country through what seemed its most dangerous periods, when American armies were fighting in nations on its borders. And it was he who had turned his back on Russia in favor of a foreign policy that meant dealing with the capitalist powers.

It was Mao who had presided over China's reemergence to take what all Chinese consider the nation's rightful place in the world. Since Mao's great victories, the idea of concessions to foreign powers in Chinese cities has been inconceivable. And it has been inconceivable since Mao that China would be a conglomeration of fiefdoms controlled by Nationalists, Communists, and warlords, rather than a single united country.

It was under Mao that life as it had been known in China since ancient days underwent drastic changes. Most of China's food comes from the communes, only a tiny percentage from the private plots, and state-run enterprises account for China's industrial output. In addition, there has been a major shift of loyalties because of Mao's policies. Not only do almost all Chinese work for the state, almost all rely on the state for far more than they ever expected of government before. There are still men and women alive who remember the days of the warlords, when the government could not be counted on for protection. And there are people alive who remember when China's infant mortality rate was one of the highest in the world and most Chinese were under the very real threat of famine. Whether or not in their hearts the Chinese underwent the changes Mao expected of them remains a question. In China under Deng it is again possible to talk openly about the ideas of Confucius, and for most Chinese traditional family units are still intact.

Yet, in the Orient it has always been possible to hold seemingly contradictory positions at the same time. It is quite possible that the Chinese today can believe in the old ways and also believe in Communism. Much has been said about how the Chinese are accustomed to wearing masks, appearing to be what is expected of them for certain occasions. Mao's insistence on constant struggle, on changing the way the people thought, was an admission that while the people might be wearing the masks of Communists, in their hearts they might still hold traditional beliefs.

Perhaps nobody will ever know the innermost thoughts of the great mass of the Chinese. And nobody can say for sure in what directions leaders of the future will take them. But whether the pragmatists run the country, or more radical elements again get the upper hand, nobody seriously believes that China after Mao will ever again be what it was before him.

FOR FURTHER READING

Carter, Peter. *Mao*. New York: Viking, 1979. (The clearest of the recent short biographies.)

Hoobler, Dorothy and Thomas. *U.S.–China Relations Since World War II*. New York: Franklin Watts, 1981. (A balanced, straightforward review of U.S.–Chinese relations, with emphasis on the period of rebuilding that followed Nixon's trip to China in 1972.)

Karnow, Stanley. *Mao and China: From Revolution to Revolution*. New York: Viking, 1972. (A lucid, if slightly dated, account of Mao's life and the Chinese Communist revolution.)

Pye, Lucian W. *Mao Tse-tung: The Man in the Leader*. New York: Basic Books, 1976. (A psychological study by a leading China scholar.)

Terrill, Rose. *Mao: A Biography*. New York: Harper & Row, 1980. By far the most comprehensive biography of Mao to date, and almost certain to be so for many years to come.

Wilson, Dick. *The People's Emperor, Mao*. New York: Doubleday, 1980. (A work by the most thorough of the popular writers on China.)

INDEX

China *(continued)*
  tions with, 50–51, 65–70, 78, 101; split in, 24–25; U.S. relations with, 49, 51, 101, 103–105
Chinese People's Political Consultative Conference, 53
Ching dynasty, 6–7
Chou En-lai, 21, 34, 38, *47*, 62, 72, 83, *88*, 95, 102, 106, 107, 108, 110
Chu Teh, 22, 25, *47*, 91, 111; and Mao, 25, 37
Commune system, 73–76, 80–81
Communism, 18; Chinese beginnings of, 18–23; Soviet, 18, 19, 24, 50–51, 60, 66, 68–70, 101; U.S. fear of, 49–50. *See also* Chinese Communist Party
Concessions, 6, 10, 12, 40; post-World War I Japanese Control, 18
Confucius, 7, 11, 54, 114; anti-Confucius drive, 108
Cultural Revolution, 80–96, 98–100, 108, 109
Czechoslovakia, 1968 Soviet invasion of, 101

Deng Xiaoping, 78, 80, 83, 92, 94, 107, 108–109, 113, 114

England, 3, 6, 81

Farming: communal, 73–76, 80–81; 1960s, 80–81
Formosa, 48; Nationalist retreat to, 48, 51. *See also* Taiwan
France, in Indochina, 3, 62, 87

Great Leap Forward, 70–73
Great Wall, 7
Guerrilla warfare, 24, 25, 32, 45, 46, 89

Hong Kong, 6, 57

Hsai-fang, 55
Hunan Province, Mao in, 11, 12, 13, 19, 21, 22
Hundred Flowers campaign, 63–65, 70, 76

India, 3, 81
Indochina, French in, 3, 62, 87
Indonesia, 3
Industrial production: and Great Leap, 72–73; 1950s, 55, 56, 62, 72; 1960s, 80, 81

Japan, 2–3, 13–15, 62; vs. Chinese, 1937–1945, 38–41, 44; in Manchuria, 29, 33, 38, 44; post-World War I control of concessions, 18

Khrushchev, Nikita, 66, *67*, 68–69
Kissinger, Henry, 104
Korea, 2–3
Korean War, 56–59, 62, 66

Land reform, 1950s, 53–55
Laos, 3
Lin Biao, 22, 34, 77, 80, 83, 84, *88*, 92, 94, 98, 99, 106; fall of, 100–103
Little Red Book, 84, 90, 100
Liu Shauqi, *52*, 64, 76, 98, 102
Long March, 30–35

Manchuria, 6, 55, 81; Japanese in, 29, 33, 38, 44; Nationalists vs. PLA for, 44, 46
Manchus, 6–7, 13, 16
Mandate of Heaven, 2, 56
Mao Zedong, *14, 31, 36, 47, 52, 88, 93*; birth of, 10; childhood of, 10–13; China affected by, 113–114; and Chu Teh, 25, 37; and Cultural Revolution, 80–96, 98–100, 108, 109; death of, 98, 108, 113; decline of, 76–78, 80,

Sun Yat-sen: Nationalist Party under, 19, 20; and 1911 revolution, 15, 16

Taiping Rebellion, 7, 12
Taiwan, 3, 48, 57; Nationalist retreat to, 48, 51. *See also* Formosa
Thailand, 3
Third World nations, 62, 68, 69, 107
Thought of Mao Zedong, 84, 85, 98, 99
Tibet, 56, 81
T'ien An Men Square, Peking, 110, *112*

United States: CCP relations with, 49, 51, 101, 103–105; in Korean War, 57–59; Nationalists supported by, 48, 49–50, 51; 1950s Soviet relations with, 68–70; Nixon/China diplomacy, 104–105; post-war communist fear of, 49–50; in Vietnam, 87, 101, 104
Urban reform, 1950s, 55–56

Vietnam, 3, 87; U.S. in, 87, 101, 104

Warlords, 17, 21, 28
Western powers, 21, 62, 68; and Boxer Rebellion, 12; mediation efforts of between CCP and Nationalist China, 40–41; nineteenth century encroachment on China, 2–3, 5–7, 12. *See also names of countries*
Women, 1950s liberation of, 54–55
World War I, 18
World War II, 40, 49

Yenan, 45; Red Army in, 33–35, *36*, 37
Yuan Shihkai, 16, 17